Collins

KS3 Maths Year 7

Workbook

Katherine Pate, Trevor Senior and Michael White

About this Workbook

There are three Collins workbooks for KS3 Maths:

Year 7 Maths ISBN 9780008553692
Year 8 Maths ISBN 9780008553708
Year 9 Maths ISBN 9780008553715

Together they provide topic-based practice for all the skills and content on the Programme of Study for Key Stage 3 Maths.

The questions for each topic have been organised into **three levels** of increasing difficulty.

Track your progress by recording your marks in the box at the end of each level and the summary box at the end of each topic.

Found throughout the book, the **QR codes** can be scanned on your smartphone. Each QR code links to a video working through the solution to one of the questions on that double page spread.

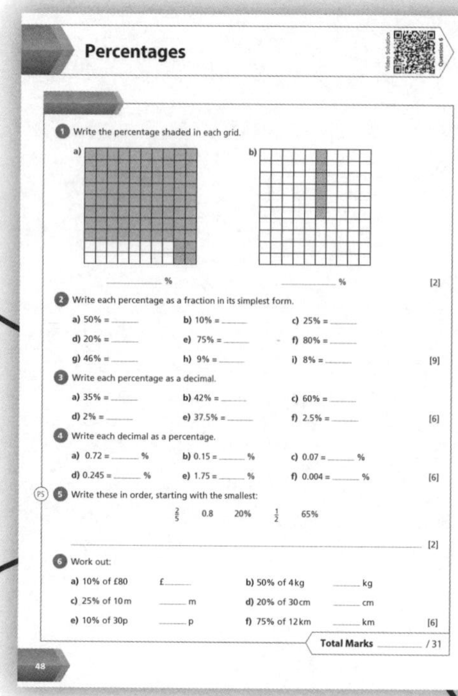

Percentages

Video Solution Question 6

1 Write the percentage shaded in each grid.

a) ______ % b) ______ % [2]

2 Write each percentage as a fraction in its simplest form.

a) 50% = ______ b) 10% = ______ c) 25% = ______
d) 20% = ______ e) 75% = ______ f) 80% = ______
g) 46% = ______ h) 9% = ______ i) 8% = ______ [9]

3 Write each percentage as a decimal.

a) 35% = ______ b) 42% = ______ c) 60% = ______
d) 2% = ______ e) 37.5% = ______ f) 2.5% = ______ [6]

4 Write each decimal as a percentage.

a) 0.72 = ______ % b) 0.15 = ______ % c) 0.07 = ______ %
d) 0.245 = ______ % e) 1.75 = ______ % f) 0.004 = ______ % [6]

(PS) 5 Write these in order, starting with the smallest:

$\frac{2}{5}$ 0.8 20% $\frac{1}{2}$ 65%

______ [2]

6 Work out:

a) 10% of £80 £______ b) 50% of 4 kg ______ kg
c) 25% of 10 m ______ m d) 20% of 30 cm ______ cm
e) 10% of 30p ______ p f) 75% of 12 km ______ km [6]

Total Marks ______ / 31

48

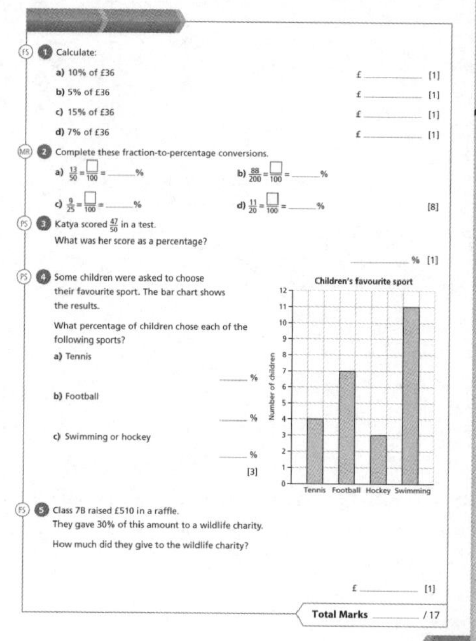

(FS) 1 Calculate:

a) 10% of £36 £ ______ [1]
b) 5% of £36 £ ______ [1]
c) 15% of £36 £ ______ [1]
d) 7% of £36 £ ______ [1]

(MR) 2 Complete these fraction-to-percentage conversions.

a) $\frac{13}{50} = \frac{\square}{100}$ = ______ % b) $\frac{88}{200} = \frac{\square}{100}$ = ______ %
c) $\frac{9}{25} = \frac{\square}{100}$ = ______ % d) $\frac{11}{20} = \frac{\square}{100}$ = ______ % [8]

(PS) 3 Katya scored $\frac{47}{50}$ in a test.
What was her score as a percentage?

______ % [1]

(PS) 4 Some children were asked to choose their favourite sport. The bar chart shows the results.

What percentage of children chose each of the following sports?

a) Tennis ______ %
b) Football ______ %
c) Swimming or hockey ______ % [3]

(FS) 5 Class 7B raised £510 in a raffle.
They gave 30% of this amount to a wildlife charity.

How much did they give to the wildlife charity?

£ ______ [1]

Total Marks ______ / 17

49

Symbols are used to highlight questions that test key **skills**:

(MR) Mathematical Reasoning

(PS) Problem Solving

(FS) Financial Skills

To show how confident you feel with these skills, colour in the symbols alongside each question and at the end of each topic:

Green = Got it!
Orange = Nearly there
Red = Needs practice

Try to answer as many questions as possible without using a calculator. You will need extra paper for workings in some questions.

Questions where calculators **must not** be used are marked with this symbol:

The **answers** are included at the back so that you can mark your own work. **Helpful tips** are also included.

Contents

Answers

ACKNOWLEDGEMENTS

The author and publisher are grateful to the copyright holders for permission to use quoted materials and images.

All images are © HarperCollins*Publishers* Limited

Every effort has been made to trace copyright holders and obtain their permission for the use of copyright material. The author and publisher will gladly receive information enabling them to rectify any error or omission in subsequent editions. All facts are correct at time of going to press.

Published by Collins
An imprint of HarperCollins*Publishers*
1 London Bridge Street
London SE1 9GF

HarperCollins*Publishers*
Macken House
39/40 Mayor Street Upper
Dublin 1
D01 C9W8
Ireland

ISBN 9780008553692

First published 2023

10 9 8 7 6 5 4 3 2 1

British Library Cataloguing in Publication Data.

A CIP record of this book is available from the British Library.

Publisher: Clare Souza
Commissioning: Richard Toms
Authors: Katherine Pate, Trevor Senior and Michael White
Editorial: Richard Toms and Amanda Dickson
Videos: Anne Stothers
Cover Design: Kevin Robbins and Sarah Duxbury
Inside Concept Design: Sarah Duxbury and Paul Oates
Text Design and Layout: Contentra Technologies
Artwork: Contentra Technologies
Production: Emma Wood
Printed in India by Multivista Global Pvt. Ltd.

This book is produced from independently certified FSC™ paper to ensure responsible forest management.

For more information visit:
www.harpercollins.co.uk/green

Number Properties

1 a) Write this number in words: 497 016

.... [1]

b) Write this number in figures:
three million, twenty-four thousand, one hundred and two

.... [1]

2 Round 824 516 to:

a) the nearest 10 .... [1]

b) the nearest thousand .... [1]

c) the nearest ten thousand .... [1]

3 Work out:

a) $\sqrt{64}$ .... b) $\sqrt{121}$ .... c) $\sqrt[3]{8}$ .... d) $\sqrt{81}$ .... [4]

4 Work out:

a) 7^2 .... b) 4^3 .... c) 12^2 .... d) 3^3 .... [4]

5 Write using powers.

a) $2 \times 2 \times 2 \times 2 \times 2 = 2^{\dots}$ b) $3 \times 3 \times 3 \times 3 = 3^{\dots}$ [2]

6 Work out:

a) $2^3 \times 5^2$ .... [2]

b) $3^2 \times 2^3$ .... [2]

c) $9^2 \times 10^2$ .... [2]

d) $2 \times 3^3 \times 5$ .... [2]

MR 7 Here is a box of numbers.

1	27	28	2	14	20	9
4	5	7	6	3	8	

From the box, write down:

a) the factors of 54 .... [2]

b) the multiples of 4 .... [2]

c) the prime factors of 28 .... [2]

MR **8** Here is a box of numbers.

15	10	18	48
42	24	36	60

From the box, write down:

a) a multiple of 2, 3 and 5 ______ [1]

b) a multiple of 3 but not of 6 ______ [1]

c) a multiple of 4 but not of 8 ______ [1]

9 **a)** Complete this prime factor decomposition of 126

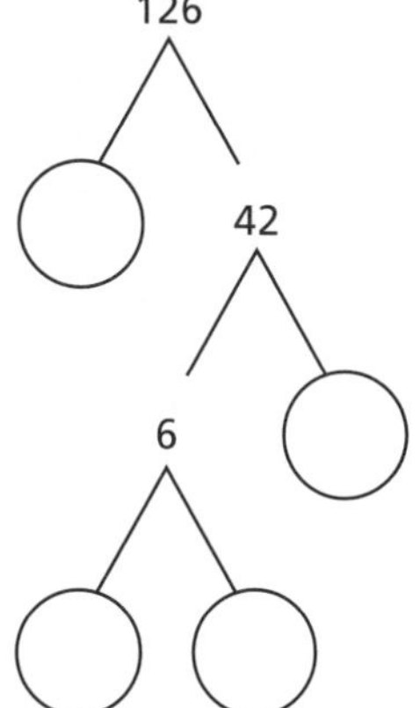

[4]

b) Write 126 as a product of prime factors. ______ [1]

Total Marks ______ / 37

MR **1** Write the number that is:

a) 1000 times smaller than 1 million ______ [1]

b) 100 times larger than 4087 ______ [1]

PS **2** Write in order, from smallest to greatest:

$\sqrt{49}$ $\sqrt{24}$ $\sqrt[3]{27}$ $\sqrt[3]{125}$ ______ [1]

MR PS **3** How many times heavier is 8 kg than 8 g? ______ [1]

4 Write each of these as a power of 2

a) 8 ______ **b)** 32 ______ **c)** 128 ______ **d)** 256 ______ [4]

PS **5** Write down the smallest number with prime factors 2, 3, 5 and 7 ______ [1]

6 Work out $5^3 - 6^2$ .... [2]

PS 7 Write in order, from longest to shortest: 2070 mm, 2.7 m, 2.07 cm, 20.07 cm, 7.02 m

.... [2]

8 Calculate an estimate of 3127 + 159 208 to the nearest thousand.

.... [2]

MR 9 The Venn diagram shows the prime factors of 1980 and 378

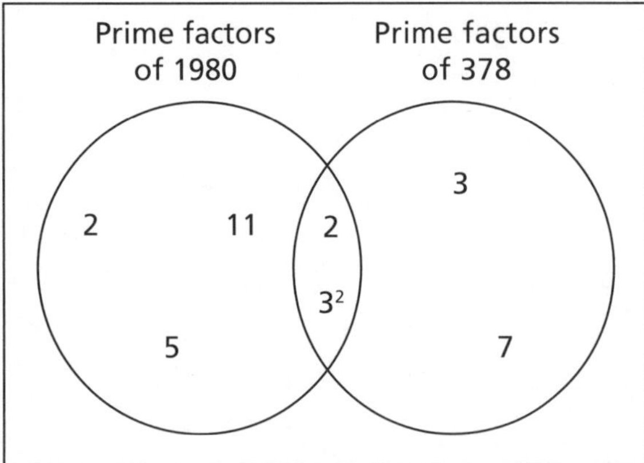

Find:

a) the highest common factor of 1980 and 378 .... [1]

b) the lowest common multiple of 1980 and 378 .... [2]

Total Marks .... / 18

MR PS 1 How many times shorter than 15 m is 3 mm?  .... [1]

PS 2 Shona has a square piece of card, with side 7 cm. She cuts a square with side 4 cm out of the centre of the card.

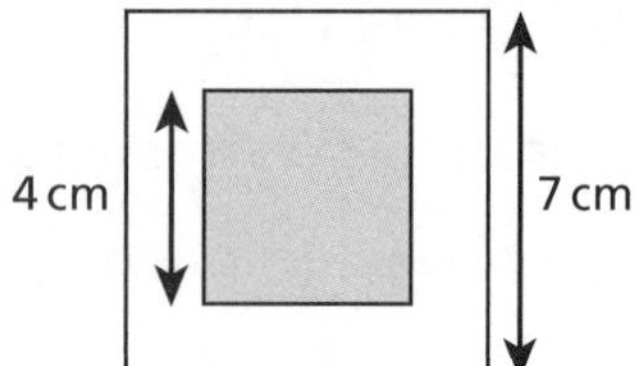

What area of card does she have left?

.... cm^2 [2]

3 Find the highest common factor of 204 and 96

.... [3]

PS **4** What is the smallest integer that is a multiple of 3, 5 and 7?

.... [1]

PS **5** What is the greatest two-digit common multiple of 3, 4 and 12?

.... [2]

PS **6** Dean lives 42 km from the office where he works. He drives to work and back every weekday.

Estimate the total distance he drives in 6 weeks, to the nearest 100 km.

.... km [2]

PS **7** When I leave the fridge door open, the fridge bleeps every 12 seconds.
When the dishwasher cycle has finished, the dishwasher bleeps every 15 seconds.
The fridge and the dishwasher both bleep at 10:00

When will they next bleep at the same time?

.... [2]

PS **8** Maisie has 84 blue counters, 132 red counters and 180 yellow counters. She wants to put all the counters into boxes so that each box has the same number of a particular colour.

a) What is the largest number of boxes Maisie can fill with counters?

.... [2]

b) How many of each colour counter will there be in each box?

Blue: .... Red: .... Yellow: .... [2]

PS **9** A sheet of paper measures 21 cm by 30 cm.

21 cm

30 cm

What is the maximum number of rectangles 3 cm by 7 cm that you can cut from this sheet of paper?

.... [2]

Total Marks .... / 19

.... / 37	
.... / 18	
.... / 19	

How do you feel about these skills?

PS MR

Green = Got it!
Orange = Nearly there
Red = Needs practice

1 Complete the inputs and outputs for each function machine. The first one has been started. 

a)

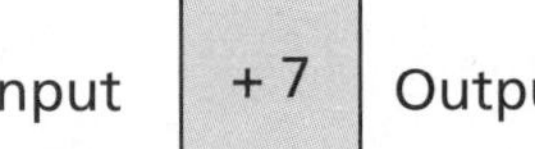

Input	+ 7	Output
2	→	9
5	→	12
9	→	___
12	→	___

b)

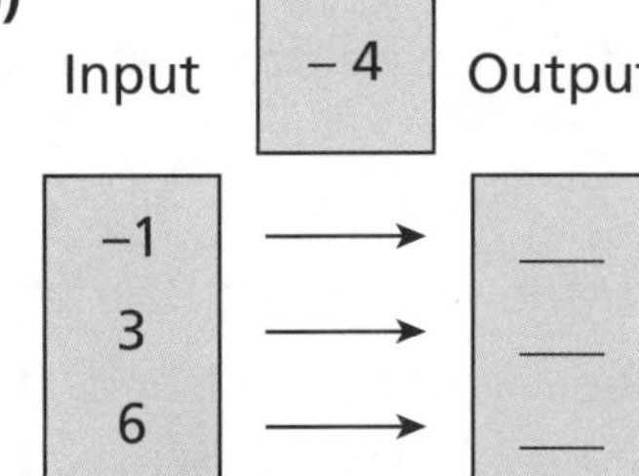

Input	− 4	Output
−1	→	___
3	→	___
6	→	___
10	→	___

c)

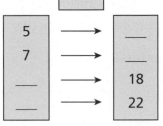

Input	× 2	Output
5	→	___
7	→	___
___	→	18
___	→	22

d)

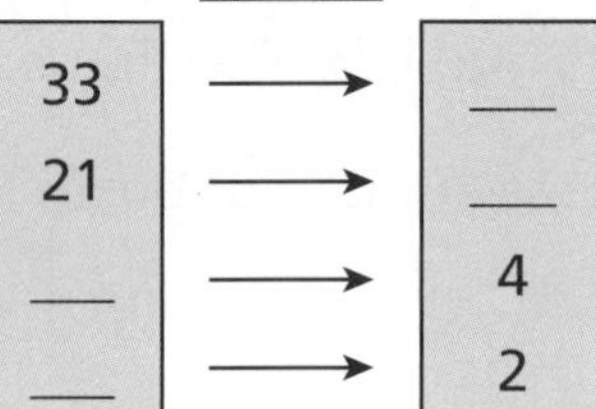

Input	÷ 3	Output
33	→	___
21	→	___
___	→	4
___	→	2

[4]

2 Work out the rule for each function machine.

a)

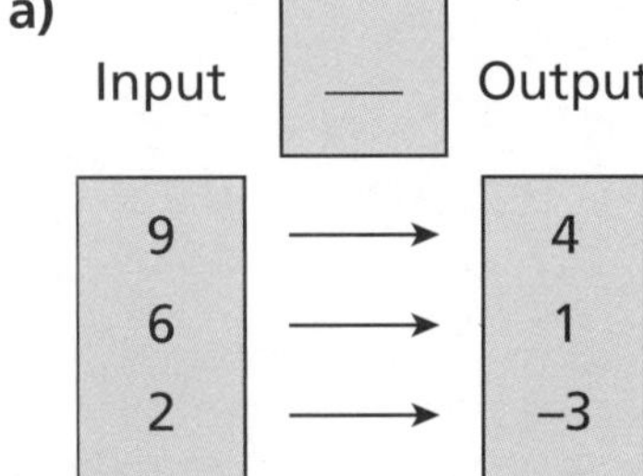

Input	___	Output
9	→	4
6	→	1
2	→	−3
0	→	−5

b)

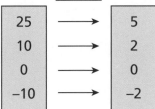

Input	___	Output
25	→	5
10	→	2
0	→	0
−10	→	−2

[2]

MR **3** Here is a number machine.

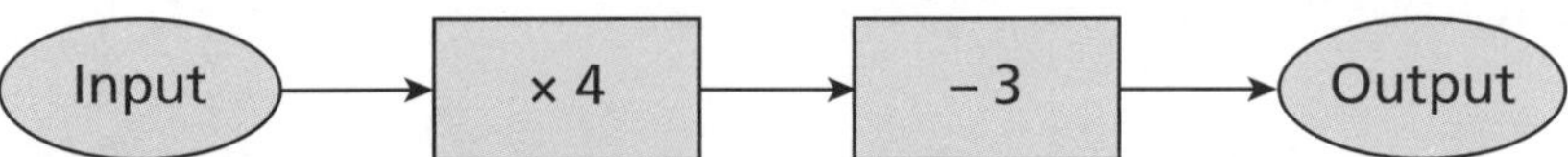

a) Work out the output when the input is 7 .... [1]

b) Work out the output when the input is −2 .... [1]

c) Work out the input when the output is 5 .... [1]

d) Work out the input when the output is 9 .... [1]

4 Use the term-to-term rule to work out the first five terms of a sequence.

The first term is given.

a) Add 12: 8, ______, ______, ______, ______ [1]

b) Subtract 9: 24, ______, ______, ______, ______ [1]

c) Multiply by 2: 1, ______, ______, ______, ______ [1]

d) Divide by 2: 32, ______, ______, ______, ______ [1]

PS 5 Sequences of patterns are made from sticks.

For each sequence, draw the next pattern of sticks and work out the number of sticks in pattern 5.

a)

Number of sticks in pattern 5 = ______ [2]

b)

Number of sticks in pattern 5 = ______ [2]

Total Marks ______ / 18

MR 1 For each sequence, write down the next two terms and the rule you used.

a) 30, 24, 18, 12, ______, ______

Rule: ______ [2]

b) 144, 72, 36, 18, ______, ______

Rule: ______ [2]

c) 1, 3, 9, 27, ______, ______

Rule: ______ [2]

d) 1.5, 3, 4.5, 6, ______, ______

Rule: ______ [2]

Sequences

Video Solution
Question 4

MR **2** Here are four sequences. 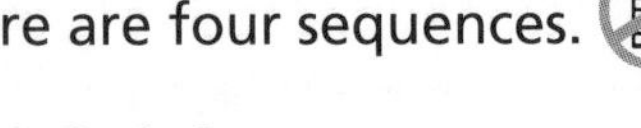

A 1, 2, 4, 8, …

B 108, 96, 84, 72, …

C 1 000 000, 100 000, 10 000, 1000, …

D $1, \frac{1}{2}, \frac{1}{4}, \frac{1}{8}, \ldots$

a) Which of the sequences will contain the number 64?

.... [1]

b) Which of the sequences will contain negative numbers?

.... [1]

c) What is the 10th number in sequence C?

.... [1]

d) Which of the sequences contain the term 0?

.... [1]

3 Here is a sequence.

7, 10, 13, 16, 19, …

Andy says the 10th term of this sequence is double the 5th term.

Explain why he is **not** correct. 

....

.... [2]

Total Marks .... / 14

 **1** The numbers in this sequence increase by 25 each time.

Write in the missing numbers. 

☐ ☐ 65 90  ☐ [2]

PS **2** A sequence starts with the number 3. The term-to-term rule is 'add 7'. 

a) Write down the first four terms of the sequence.

.... [1]

b) Jack says, "I will add together the terms of the sequence until my total reaches 100."

How many terms does he need to add together? Show your working.

....

.... [2]

PS **3** Look at this pattern of numbers.

1	$= 1 = 1^2$
$1 + 3$	$= 4 = 2^2$
$1 + 3 + 5$	$= 9 = 3^2$
$1 + 3 + 5 + 7$	$= 16 = 4^2$

a) Write down the next line of the pattern.

.... [1]

b) Use the pattern to write down the sum of the first 10 odd numbers.

.... [1]

MR **4** Here are two sequences.

71, 63, 55, 47, ... 2.5, 5, 7.5, 10, ...

Which number will appear in both sequences? 

.... [3]

Total Marks .... / 10

	.... / 18
	.... / 14
	.... / 10

How do you feel about these skills?

Green = Got it!
Orange = Nearly there
Red = Needs practice

Perimeter and Area

Video Solution Question 6

1. This triangle has a perimeter of 36 mm.

   Work out the missing length.

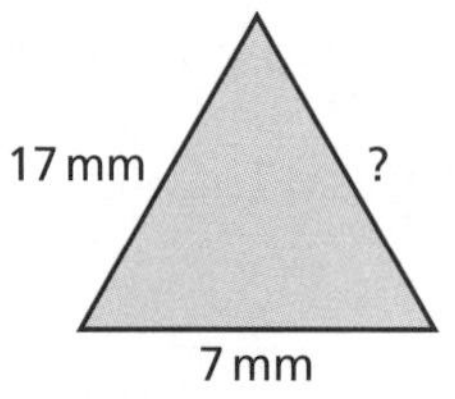

   17 mm, ?, 7 mm

   .... mm [1]

2. Work out the total perimeter of these two rectangles.

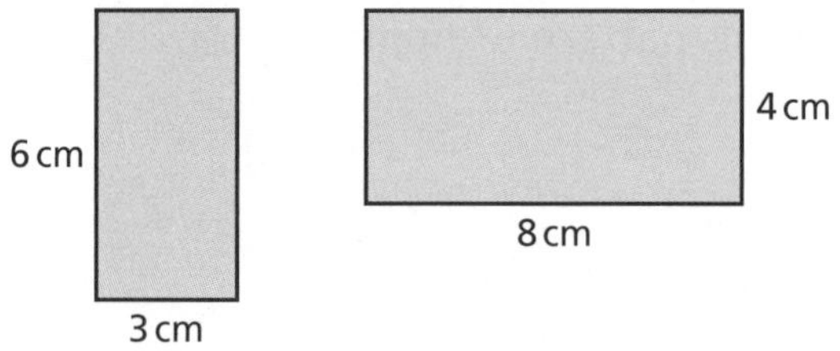

   6 cm, 3 cm; 4 cm, 8 cm

   .... cm [2]

3. Each square in the grid represents $1\,cm^2$.

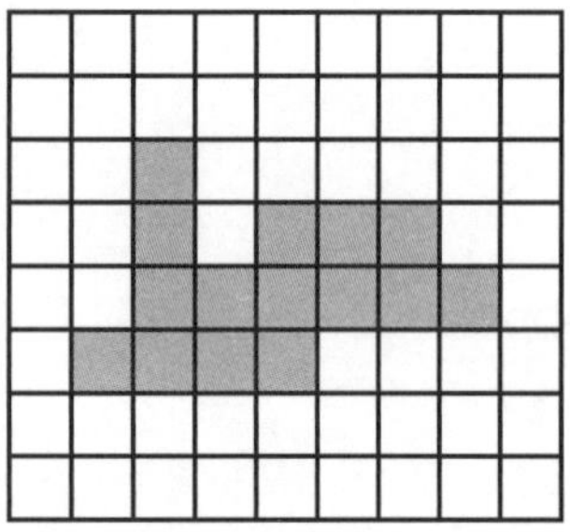

   Work out the perimeter and the area of the shaded shape.

   Perimeter: .... cm Area: .... cm^2 [2]

MR 4. A regular pentagon has five equal sides. The perimeter of the pentagon is 45 cm.

   Find the length of one side of the pentagon.

   .... cm [1]

5. Here are two rectangles, P and Q.

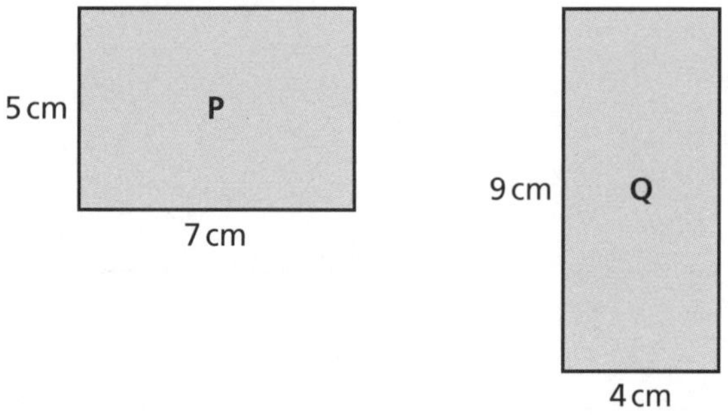

   P: 5 cm, 7 cm

   Q: 9 cm, 4 cm

   a) Which rectangle has the larger area and by how much?

   .... [3]

   b) Which rectangle has the larger perimeter and by how much?

   .... [3]

MR **6** A square has a perimeter of 28 mm.

Work out:

a) the length of one side of the square

.... mm [1]

b) the area of the square

.... mm^2 [1]

7 Work out the area of this triangle.

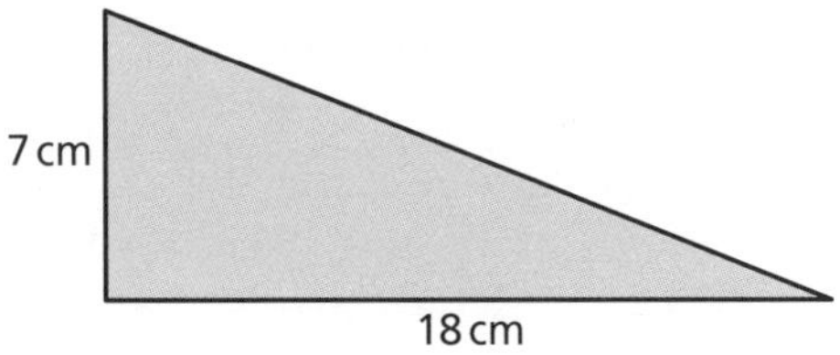

7 cm

18 cm

.... cm^2 [1]

Total Marks .... / 15

MR **1** A rectangle has length 8 mm and perimeter 28 mm.

Find the area of the rectangle. .... mm^2 [2]

MR **2** Rectangle B is 3 cm longer and 3 cm wider than rectangle A.

Work out the total area of the two rectangles.

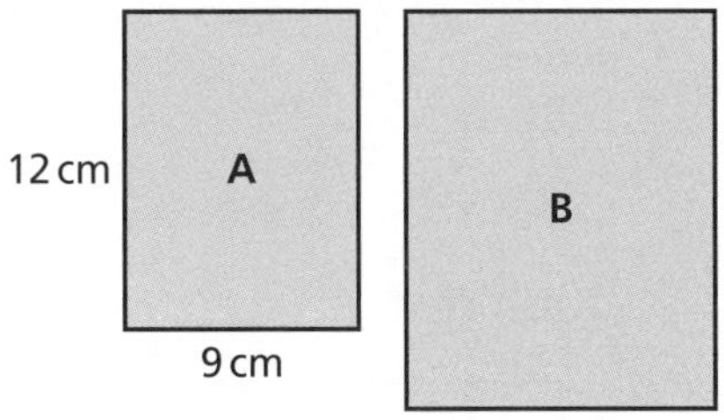

12 cm A

9 cm

B

.... cm^2 [3]

3 Work out the area of the trapezium and the area of the parallelogram.

a)

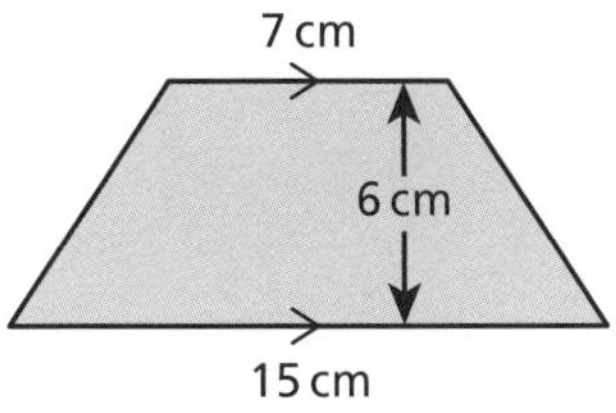

7 cm

6 cm

15 cm

Area: .... cm^2 [2]

b)

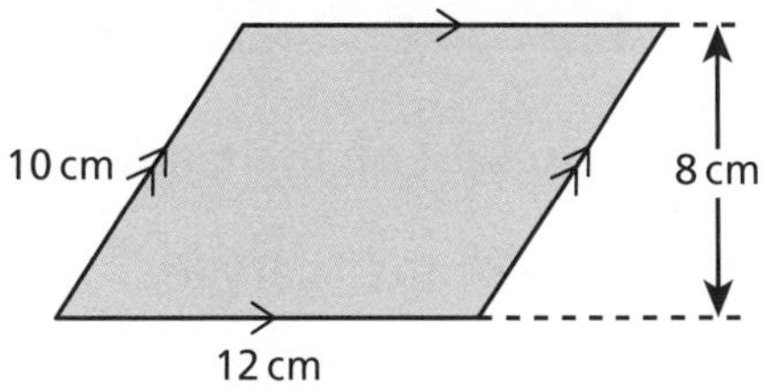

10 cm

8 cm

12 cm

Area: .... cm^2 [2]

Video Solution Question 6

MR **4** Duska needs to work out the area of the triangle.

She multiplies 6 by 10 then halves the answer because it is a triangle.

Her answer is 30 cm^2.

Explain clearly what mistake Duska has made.

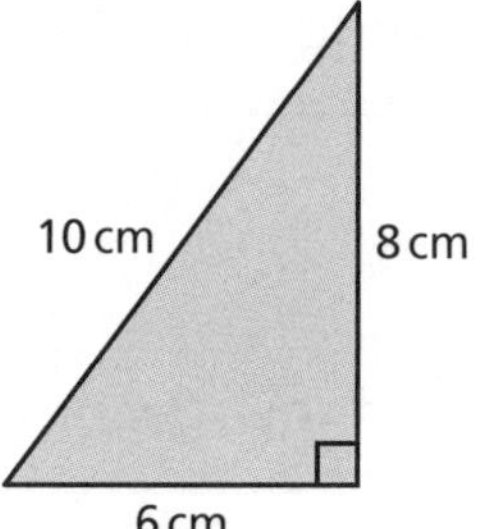

[2]

PS **5** Find the area of the grey shaded region.

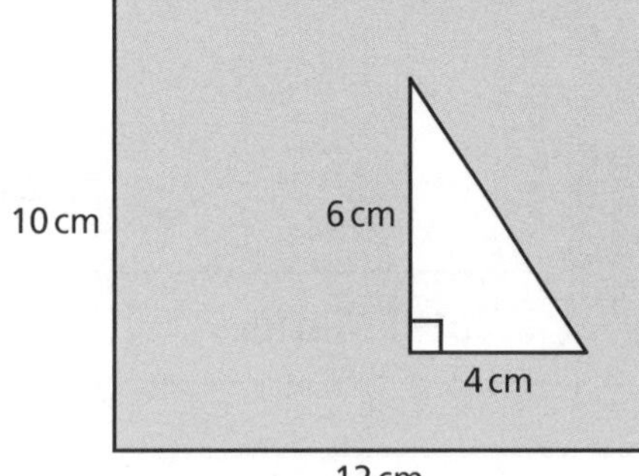

cm^2 [3]

MR PS FS **6** A gardener has a square lawn with an area of 36 m^2. The gardener wants to put fencing completely around the lawn. The fencing costs £9 per metre.

a) Work out the perimeter of the lawn.

Perimeter: ________ m [2]

b) Work out the total cost of the fencing.

Total cost: £ ________ [1]

Total Marks ________ / 17

MR **1** A triangle has a height of 16 cm and an area of 72 cm^2.

Work out the base of the triangle.

________ cm [2]

2 Find the area of each shape below.

a)

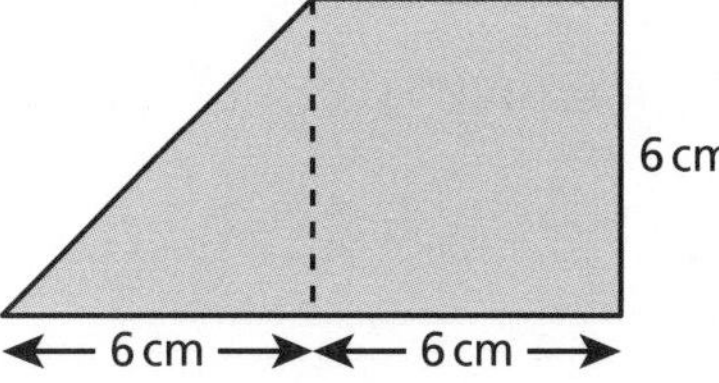

b)

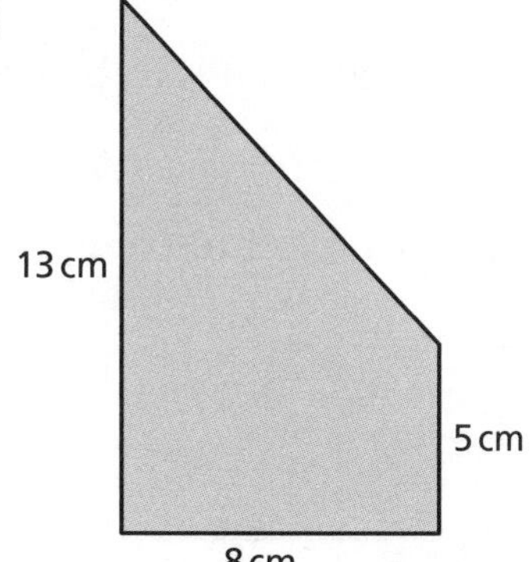

.... cm^2 [2]

.... cm^2 [2]

MR **3** Find the perimeter and area of these composite shapes.

a)

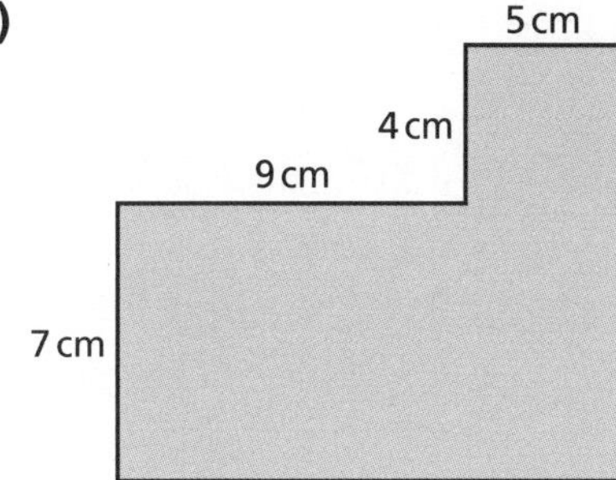

Perimeter: .... cm

Area: .... cm^2 [4]

b)

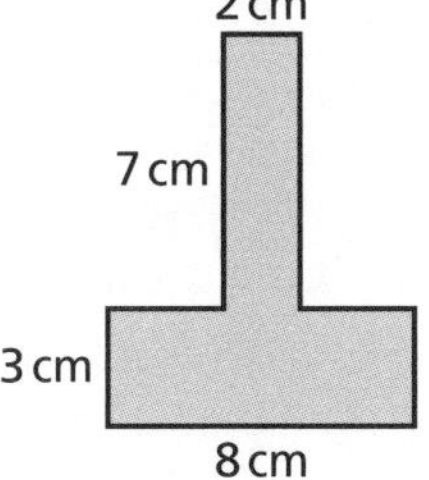

Perimeter: .... cm

Area: .... cm^2 [4]

c)

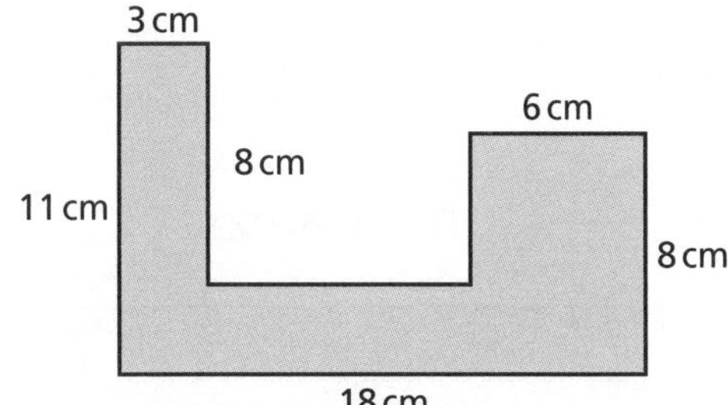

Perimeter: .... cm

Area: .... cm^2 [4]

Perimeter and Area

Video Solution Question 6

(PS) (FS) **4** The diagram shows a floor that is to be completely painted. One tin of paint costing £20 covers $4\,m^2$.

What will be the cost of paint to complete this job?

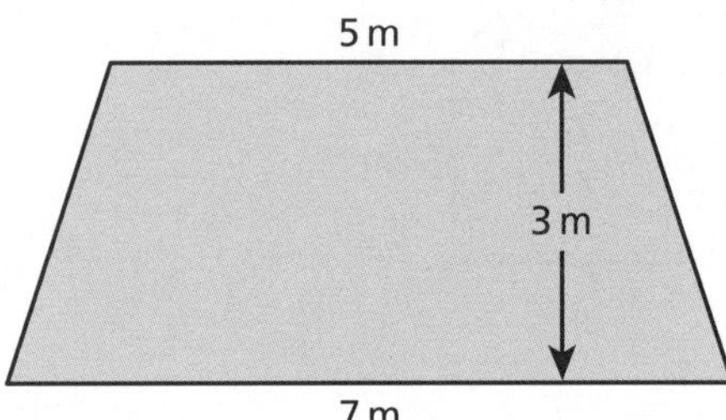

£ .... [3]

(MR) **5** Work out the area of the unshaded region.

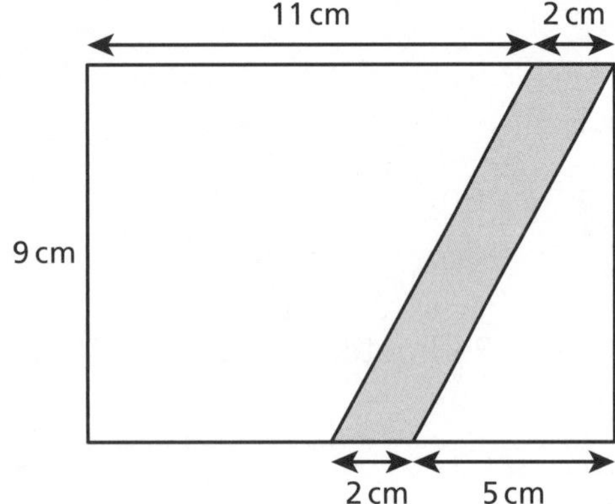

.... cm^2 [4]

(MR) **6** This trapezium has an area of $28\,cm^2$ and a perimeter of 24 cm.

Work out the length of n.

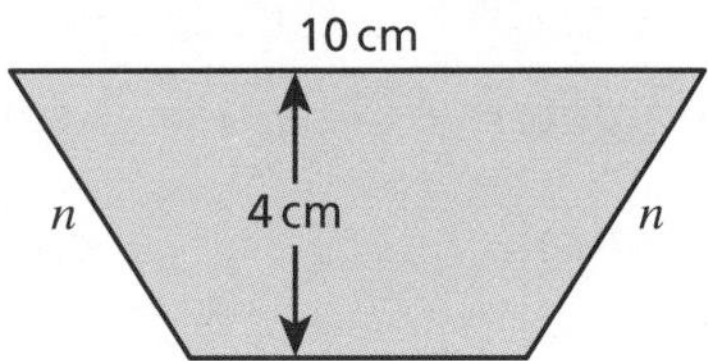

.... cm [4]

Total Marks .... / 29

....	/ 15
....	/ 17
....	/ 29

How do you feel about these skills?

Green = Got it!
Orange = Nearly there
Red = Needs practice

Decimal Numbers

Video Solution Question 3

1 a) What is the value of the digit 9 in 34.92? .... [1]

b) What is the value of the digit 6 in 235.46? .... [1]

2 Round 267.835 to:

a) the nearest integer .... [1]

b) the nearest tenth .... [1]

c) the nearest hundredth .... [1]

3 The numbers in the circles sum to the total at the top.

Write in the missing numbers.

a) 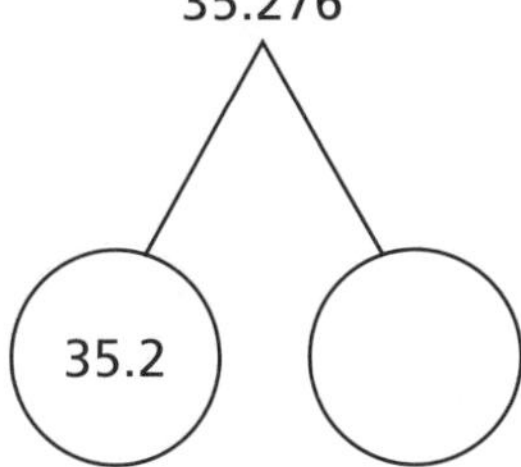

b) 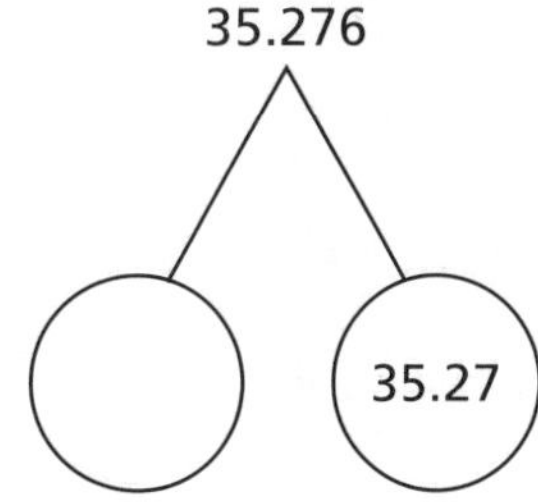

c) 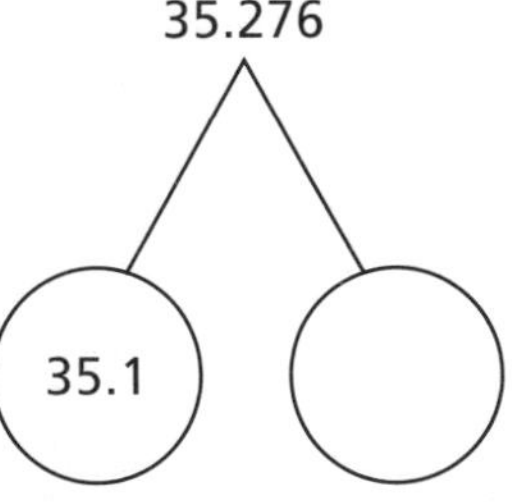

d) 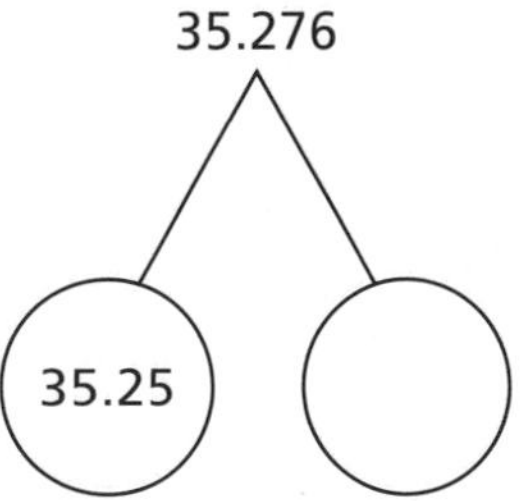

[4]

4 Work out: 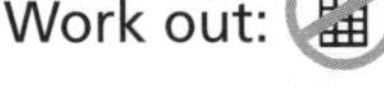

a) 0.37×100 .... b) 1.54×1000 .... c) 0.02×10 ....

d) $342 \div 1000$ .... e) 5.007×100 .... f) $0.59 \div 10$ ....

g) 6.025×10 .... h) $5 \div 100$ .... i) 0.009×100 .... [9]

5 Write in order, starting with the smallest:

3.2 3.09 3.271 3.15 3.146 3.4

.... [2]

6 Complete these statements. 

a) $0.1 = \frac{1}{\square}$ b) $0.01 = \frac{1}{\square}$ c) $0.001 = \frac{1}{\square}$ [3]

Decimal Numbers

7 Round 15.645 to:

a) 2 decimal places .... [1]

b) 1 decimal place .... [1]

8 Convert each measurement into the unit shown.

a) 4.35 m = ... cm **b)** 1.6 litres = ... ml **c)** 250 g = ... kg

d) 1500 m = ... km **e)** 3650 ml = ... litres **f)** 4.8 kg = ... g

g) 176 kg = ... tonnes **h)** 850 mm = ... m **i)** 14 260 m = ... km [9]

Total Marks .... / 34

MR 1 Write the number that is:

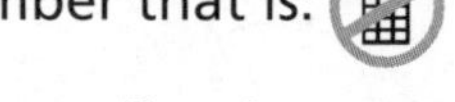

a) 1000 times smaller than 245

.... [1]

b) 100 times larger than 0.06

.... [1]

MR 2 Write the missing digits in these calculations.

a)

	4	7	•	3	2	6
+		9	•	☐	9	☐
	5	☐	•	4	☐	1

b)

	5	1	☐	•	1	2	☐
–	2	4	1	•	3	8	6
	2	7	1	•	☐	3	9

[7]

MR 3 How many times greater than 0.05 is 5000?

.... [1]

MR 4 Complete these statements.

a) Multiplying by 0.1 is equivalent to dividing by .... [1]

b) Multiplying by 0.001 is equivalent to dividing by .... [1]

c) Dividing by 0.1 is equivalent to multiplying by .... [1]

d) Dividing by 0.01 is equivalent to multiplying by .... [1]

5 Work out:

a) 12×0.1 .... b) 3.2×0.01 .... c) 65×0.001 ....

d) $56 \div 0.1$ .... e) 2.7×0.1 .... f) $0.07 \div 0.01$ ....

g) 529×0.001 .... h) $8 \div 0.001$ .... i) $0.004 \div 0.1$ .... [9]

FS **6** Estimate the total cost of 5.7 metres of fabric at £19.80 per metre.

£ .... [2]

7 Work out:

a) 0.3×7 .... b) $5.6 \div 8$ .... c) 0.16×0.2 ....

d) $0.24 \div 3$ .... e) $0.048 \div 6$ .... f) $13.2 \div 11$ ....

g) 5×0.09 .... h) $0.64 \div 8$ .... i) 6×0.05 .... [9]

MR **8** Use the multiplication fact $38 \times 127 = 4826$ to work out:

a) 3.8×127 .... b) 3.8×12.7 ....

c) 1.27×38 .... d) 0.38×127 ....

e) 3.8×1.27 .... f) 12.7×0.38 .... [6]

Total Marks .... / 40

MR PS **1** How many times shorter than 6 km is 3 cm?

.... [1]

PS **2** The scale on map is 1 cm represents 10 km.

a) A path is 7 km long.

How long is this path on the map? .... cm [1]

b) A road on the map is 3.5 cm long.

How long is this road? .... km [1]

FS **3** 20 kg of concrete costs £7.85

Work out the cost of 1 tonne of this concrete.

£ .... [2]

4 Work out: 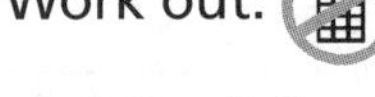

a) 2.6 × 0.5 ....

b) 4.9 ÷ 0.7 ....

c) 1.6 × 0.2 ....

d) 0.24 ÷ 0.03 ....

e) 13.6 × 0.1 ....

f) 0.35 × 0.01 ....

g) 0.3 × 0.09 ....

h) 1.6 ÷ 0.02 ....

i) 0.02 × 0.05 .... [9]

FS 5 Estimate the total cost of 29 litres of juice, at £0.51 per litre. 

£ .... [2]

MR 6 Use the multiplication fact 2.7 × 136 = 367.2 to work out:

a) 27 × 136 ....

b) 367.2 ÷ 2.7 ....

c) 3672 ÷ 2.7 ....

d) 367.2 ÷ 13.6 ....

e) 367.2 ÷ 1.36 ....

f) 3.672 ÷ 13.6 .... [6]

PS 7 One litre of floor paint covers 3.8 m^2.

Estimate the number of 1-litre cans of paint you need to paint this floor. 

5.3 m

2.8 m

.... [3]

Total Marks .... / 25

....	/ 34
....	/ 40
....	/ 25

How do you feel about these skills?

Green = Got it!
Orange = Nearly there
Red = Needs practice

Working with Numbers

Video Solution Question 4

1 Work out: 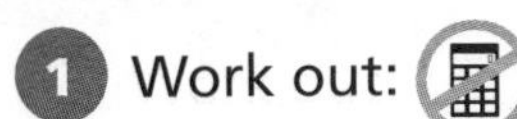

a) $-1 - 5$ .... **b)** $-3 + 2$ .... **c)** $3 - 7$ ....

d) $-22 + 15$ .... **e)** $27 - 35$ .... **f)** $-9 + 12$ .... [6]

2 Work out: 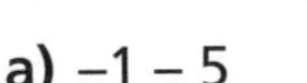

a) 348×36 **b)** 2397×114

.... [2]

3 Work out: 

a) $247 \div 4$ **b)** $862 \div 25$

.... [2]

4 Work out: 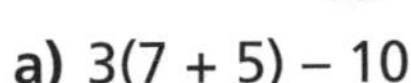

a) $3(7 + 5) - 10$ .... **b)** $6^2 - 17 + 3$ ....

c) $15 \div 3 + 2$ .... **d)** $5\sqrt{81} - 2 \times 7$ ....

e) $(8 - 6) \times (4 + 3)^2$ .... **f)** $31 - 3^3 + 5 \times 7$ .... [6]

5 One day in March, the day temperature in the Gobi Desert was 5°C, and the night temperature was –12°C.

What was the difference between the day and night temperatures?

.... °C [1]

Video Solution Question 8

FS 6 Four people share a taxi fare of £26.80 equally.

How much does each person pay?

£ .... [1]

7 Write the next three terms in this sequence:

23, 17, 11, ..., ..., ... [3]

Total Marks .... / 21

1 Work out:

a) 2 – –5 ....
b) –3 – 4 ....
c) 6 + –7 ....
d) –5 – –9 ....
e) 8 + –10 ....
f) 15 – –4 .... [6]

2 Work out:

a) 11.6 × 1.2
b) 8.25 × 15.2

.... [2]

3 Work out:

a) 62.8 ÷ 0.4
b) 55.4 ÷ 1.6

.... [2]

4 Work out:

a) 24 × 99
b) 37 × 101
c) 45 × 999

.... [3]

FS **5** Calculate the total cost of 3.6 kg of cherries at £1.49 per kilogram.

Give your answer to a suitable degree of accuracy.

£ .... [2]

6 Work out:

a) $(-2)^2$ .... **b)** $(-4)^3$ .... **c)** $\sqrt[3]{-8}$ .... [3]

7 Work out:

a) -2×7 ....

b) -3×-12 ....

c) $-25 \div 5$ ....

d) $18 \div -6$ ....

e) $-28 \div -7$ ....

f) $4 \times -8 \div -2$ .... [6]

PS **8** A train leaves London at 15:26 and arrives in Milan, Italy, at 02:06 the next morning.

How long does the train journey from London to Milan take?

.... [1]

Total Marks .... / 25

1 Work out:

a) $4763 \div 5 \div 2$ .... [1]

b) 4.9×99 .... [1]

c) $(3 - 7)^2 + 15 \div 3$ .... [1]

FS **2** Molly makes jam to sell.

To make 10 kg of jam, she needs 5 kg of strawberries, 5 kg of sugar and 2 lemons.

Empty 1 kg jam jars cost 65p each.

Strawberries cost £2.30 per kg.

Sugar costs 80p per kg

Lemons cost 37p each.

Work out the total cost of the ingredients and the jars for 20 kg of jam.

£ .... [4]

Video Solution Question 5

PS 3 A large water bottle contains 15 litres of water.

How many 330 ml cups can you fill from this water bottle?

.... [2]

MR 4 Fill in the gaps to make these calculations correct.

a) $7 + 3 - 4 -$ .... $= 0$ [1]

b) $15 - 20 + 3 +$ .... $= -1$ [1]

c) $6 \times -3 + (2 \times$ ....$) = 0$ [1]

d) $36 \div -4 + (-5)^2 -$ .... $= 2$ [1]

PS 5 The diagram shows a badge made from a regular pentagon joined to a square.

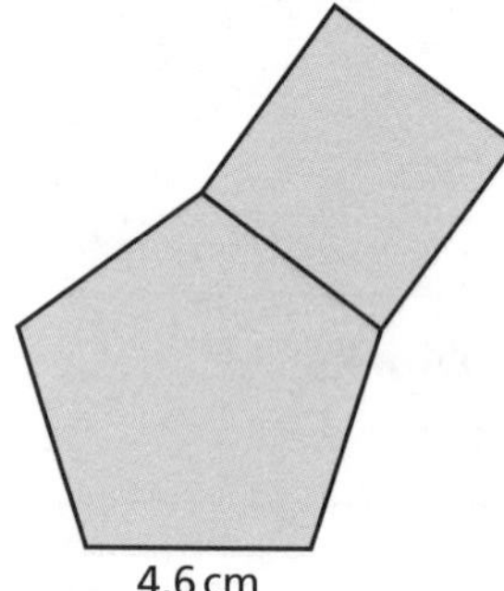

Work out the perimeter of this badge.

.... cm [2]

PS 6 Calculate the volume of a cube with side length 3.2 cm. Give your answer to 1 decimal place.

.... cm^3 [2]

Total Marks .... / 17

.... / 21	
.... / 25	
.... / 17	

How do you feel about these skills?

PS MR FS

Green = Got it!
Orange = Nearly there
Red = Needs practice

Video Solution Question 3

1 The table shows the average temperatures in a town at midnight and midday for the four seasons in one year.

	Midnight	Midday
Spring	7°C	11°C
Summer	11°C	16°C
Autumn	9°C	12°C
Winter	–3°C	4°C

a) At midnight, on average, how many degrees colder was it in winter than summer?

.... ° [1]

b) In which season was the average temperature 7 degrees warmer at midday than midnight?

.... [1]

2 The tally chart shows how 50 students travel to school.

Two more students cycle to school. Include these in the tally chart and complete the final column.

Type of travel	Tally	Number of students
Walk	卌 卌 卌	
Cycle	||||	
Bus	卌 卌 卌 卌 |||	
Car	卌 |||	

[3]

PS **3** The table shows the number of people in four quiz teams. The organiser insists that the teams should all have the same number of people.

Team	A	B	C	D
Number of people	5	9	4	10

How many people have to move out of team D, if everyone is still in one of the four teams?

.... [2]

Total Marks .... / 7

Video Solution Question 4

MR FS **1** The table shows the number of meals sold by a café on four days of one week.

Tuesday	Wednesday	Thursday	Friday
20	35	15	25

a) Show the information on a pictogram.

Tuesday	
Wednesday	
Thursday	
Friday	

Key: ◯ **represents 10 meals** [2]

b) The café is open from Monday to Friday. The number of meals sold on Monday was the same as on Wednesday.

How many meals were sold altogether that week?

.... [2]

c) On average, each meal costs £9.50

Work out the total amount taken in sales that week.

£ .... [2]

FS PS **2** Adult tickets for a football match cost £35
Child tickets cost £10

How much more does it cost for 3 adults and 2 children than for 2 adults and 3 children?

£ .... [3]

3 The bar chart shows the number of people attending a cinema over four days.

For each statement, say whether it is **true** or **false**.

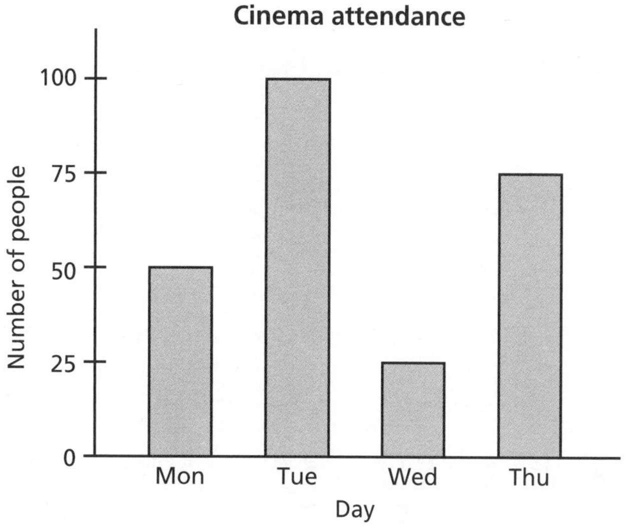

a) Altogether there were 250 people attending over the four days.

.... [1]

b) The total number of people attending on Monday and Wednesday is the same as attending on Thursday.

.... [1]

c) There were twice as many people attending on Monday than on Tuesday.

.... [1]

d) There were three times as many people attending on Thursday than on Wednesday.

.... [1]

Cinema attendance

MR **4** The table shows information about the heights (to the nearest cm) of 50 plants.

Height of plants (cm)	Number of plants
1–10	7
11–20	16
21–30	19
31–40	8

a) Draw a bar chart on the grid to represent this information. [2]

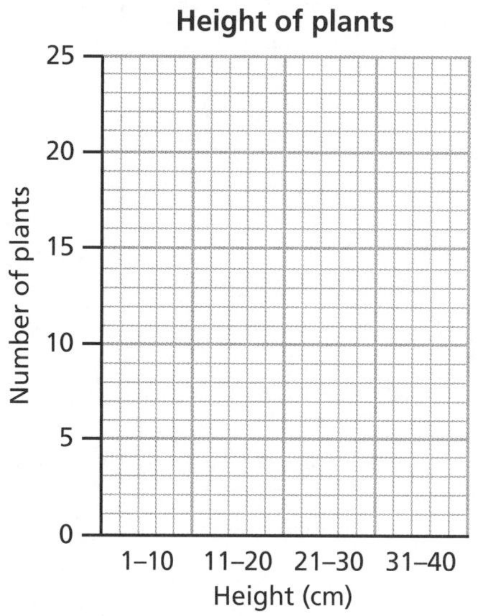

b) Which class has the most plants?

.... [1]

c) Uma says, "There are 8 plants that are taller than 35 cm."

Explain why she could be correct.

....

....

.... [1]

Height of plants

Video Solution Question 3

MR **5** **a)** Work out the mean of 1, 2, 4, 6, 8, 9

.... [2]

b) Work out the mean of 11, 12, 14, 16, 18, 19

.... [2]

c) What do you notice about your answers to parts a) and b)?

.... [1]

MR **6** The table shows the 10 test scores for two students.

Asif	8	9	5	6	2	4	3	7	6	6
Beth	3	10	10	2	5	2	3	4	10	2

a) Work out the mean score for Asif.

.... [2]

b) Work out the mean score for Beth.

.... [2]

c) Who had the better scores? .... [1]

Total Marks .... / 27

MR FS **1** The table shows the colours and makes of car in a car park.

	Silver	Black	White	Other	Total
Ford	8	11		9	38
VW	12		8		
Toyota		5		10	25
Other	13	16	11	7	
Total	40			30	140

a) Complete the table. [4]

b) How many more black cars were there than white cars in the car park?

.... [1]

c) Half of the drivers paid £1.80 for parking tickets and the rest paid £4.

How much money was taken from selling parking tickets?

£ .... [2]

2 The bar chart shows the rainfall over three months in a town.

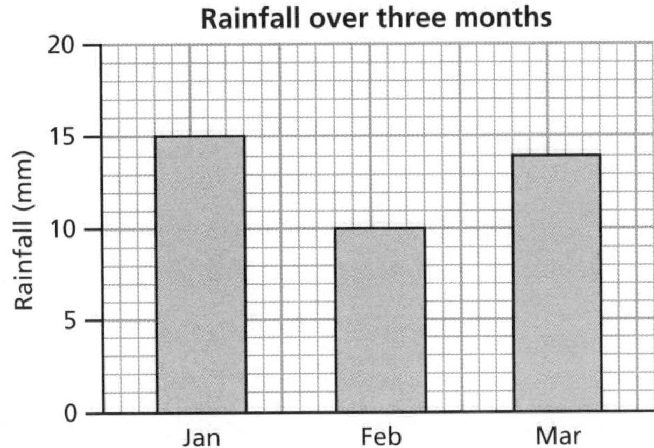

a) Work out the total rainfall over the three months.

.... mm [2]

b) When April's rainfall is included, the total rainfall for the four months is 40 mm.

What can you say about the amount of rainfall in April? Give a reason for your answer.

....

.... [2]

c) How much more rainfall was there in January than February?

.... mm [1]

PS **3** Here are five numbers. The largest of the numbers is 10.

$x + 1$	$x + 4$	$x + 8$	$x + 1$	$x + 6$

a) Work out the value of x.

$x =$ .... [2]

b) Write down the five numbers and work out the mean of them.

.... [3]

Total Marks .... / 17

	.... / 7
	.... / 27
	.... / 17

How do you feel about these skills?

PS MR FS

Green = Got it!
Orange = Nearly there
Red = Needs practice

Algebra

Video Solution Question 3

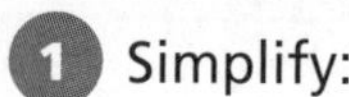

1 Simplify:

a) $a + a + a$ .... [1]

b) $a + b + b + b + a - b + a$ .... [1]

c) $4x - 4x$ .... [1]

d) $3x + 5x$ .... [1]

e) $3xy + 5xy$ .... [1]

f) $2x + 3y - 2x + 3y$ .... [1]

g) $4x^2 + 3y - 2x^2 - 4y$

.... [2]

2 Draw lines to match the equivalent algebraic expressions.
The first one has been done for you.

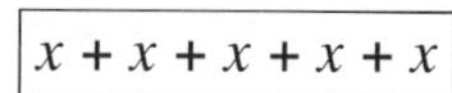

$x + x + x + x + x$	$3x + y + 2x - x$	$3x - 2x$	$4y - 2x + y - x$	$5x + x - y$

x	$4x + y$	$5x$	$6x - y$	$-3x + 5y$

[3]

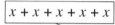

PS **3** Work out the missing coefficients.

a) $5x + \square y - \square x + 9y = 2x + 11y$

[2]

b) $9a + 4b - 3c - \square a - \square b + 4c = 6a - 2b + \square$

[3]

4 Work out the value of each expression when $a = 4$, $b = 2$ and $c = 1$

a) $6a$ .... [1]

b) $b - 7$ .... [1]

c) $a + b + c$ .... [1]

d) $3(a + 5)$ .... [1]

e) $2a + 3b - 4c$

.... [2]

5 Simplify:

a) $2 \times y$ .... [1]

b) $y \times y$ .... [1]

c) $2y \times y$ .... [1]

d) $2y \times 3y$ .... [1]

e) $2 \times y \times z$ .... [1]

f) $x \times y \times z$ .... [1]

g) $3x \times 4y \times 5z$ .... [1]

h) $t \times t \times t \times t \times t$ .... [1]

6 Write an expression for the perimeter of each shape. Write your answers as simply as possible.

a)

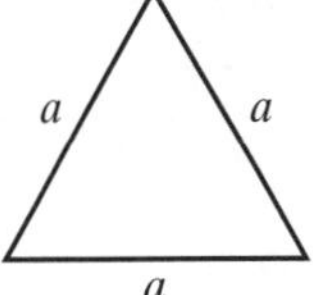

....

b)

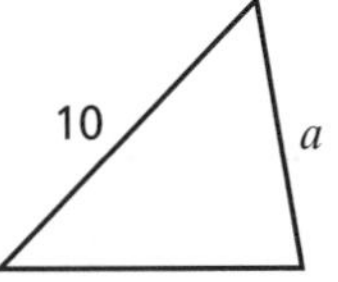

....

c)

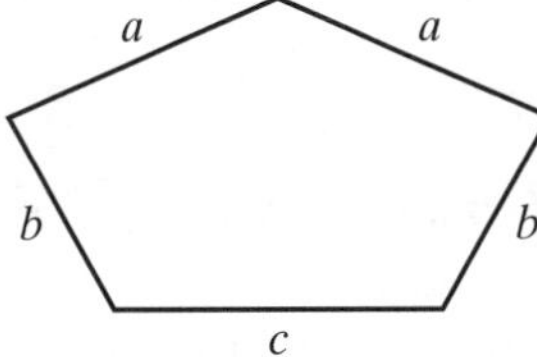

....

d)

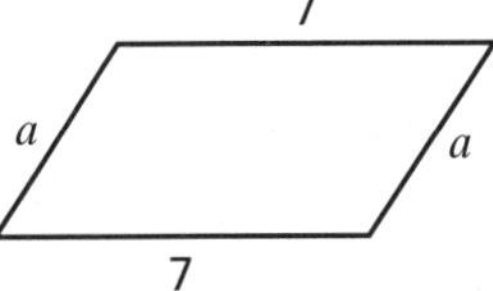

....

e)

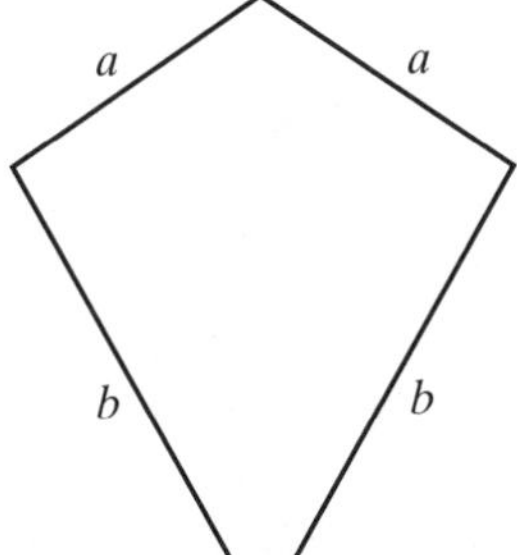

....

f)

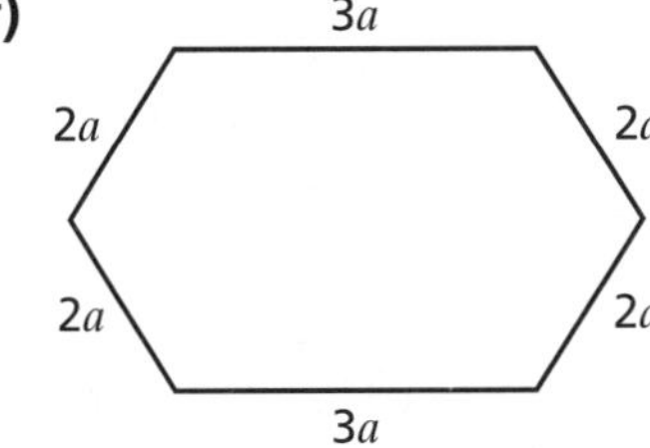

.... [6]

7 The formula for working out the perimeter, P, of a rectangle is $P = 2(l + w)$, where l is the length and w is the width.

a) Use the formula to work out the perimeter of a rectangle with $l = 4$ cm and $w = 5$ cm. .... cm [2]

b) Use the formula to work out the perimeter of a rectangle measuring 6 cm by 8 cm. .... cm [2]

c) The perimeter of a different rectangle is 24 cm.

Use the formula to work out **two** possible pairs of lengths for l and w.

$l =$ .... cm and $w =$ .... cm **or**

$l =$ .... cm and $w =$ .... cm [2]

FS **8** A cleaner works out her charge, C(£), using this formula:
$C = 13h$ where h is the number of hours worked

Calculate the charge for working:

a) 3 hours £ .... [1]

b) 4.5 hours £ .... [1]

Total Marks .... / 44

1 m is the number of minutes and h is the number of hours.

Which of the following show the relationship between the number of hours and the number of minutes?

$m = 60h$ $h = 60m$ $m = \frac{h}{60}$ $h = \frac{m}{60}$

.... and .... [2]

2 g is the number of grams and k is the number of kilograms.

Which of the following shows the relationship between the number of grams and the number of kilograms? Explain your answer.

$k = 100g$ $k = 1000g$ $g = 100k$ $g = 1000k$

....

.... [1]

MR **3** In a quiz, points are scored as follows:

2 points for each correct answer, c

–1 point for each wrong answer, w

0 points for each non-attempt, n

a) Which formula gives the total number of points, T, scored by a team? Circle your answer.

$T = c + w + n$ $\quad$ $T = 2c + w$ $\quad$ $T = 2c - w$ [1]

b) The quiz has 20 questions.

Team Grey answer 11 questions correctly, 4 questions incorrectly and the remaining questions are not attempted.

Team Blue answer 13 questions correctly and 7 questions incorrectly.

Which team scored more points? Show your working.

.... [3]

4 Use the distributive law to write equivalent expressions for each of the following.

a) $4(x + 6)$ .... [1]

b) $40(x + 6)$ .... [1]

c) $4x(x + 6)$ .... [1]

d) $4xy(x + 6)$ .... [1]

5 Here is an addition number wall. The number in each brick is the sum of the numbers in the two bricks below it.

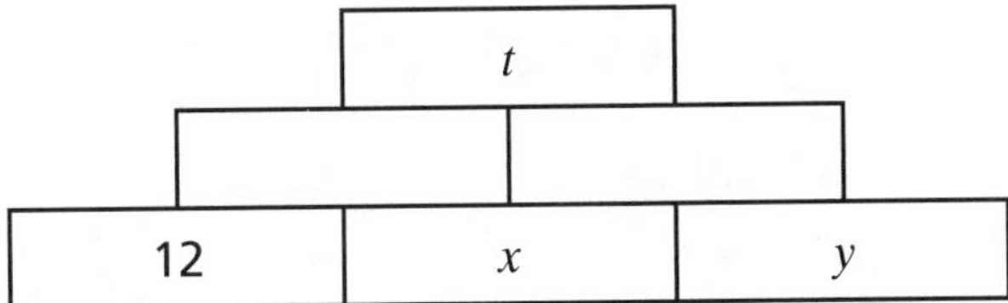

a) Work out a formula for the top number, t, in terms of x and y.

.... [2]

b) Work out the value of t if $x = 3$ and $y = 4$

$t =$ .... [2]

c) Work out the value of t if $x = 2$ and $y = -3$

$t =$ .... [2]

Total Marks .... / 17

Video Solution Question 3

1 Here is an addition number wall. The number in each brick is the sum of the numbers in the two bricks below it.

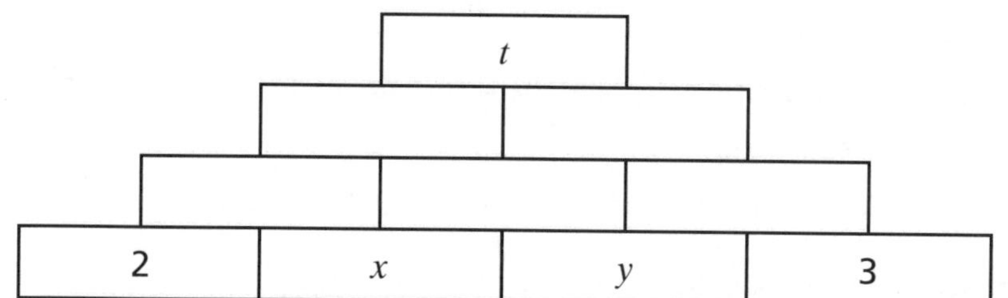

a) Work out a formula for the top number, t, in terms of x and y.

.... [2]

b) Work out the value of t if $x = 5$ and $y = 2$

$t =$ .... [2]

c) Work out the value of t if $x = 4$ and $y = 4$

$t =$ .... [2]

2 Fill in the missing expressions in this addition number wall. The expression in each brick is the sum of the values in the two bricks below it.

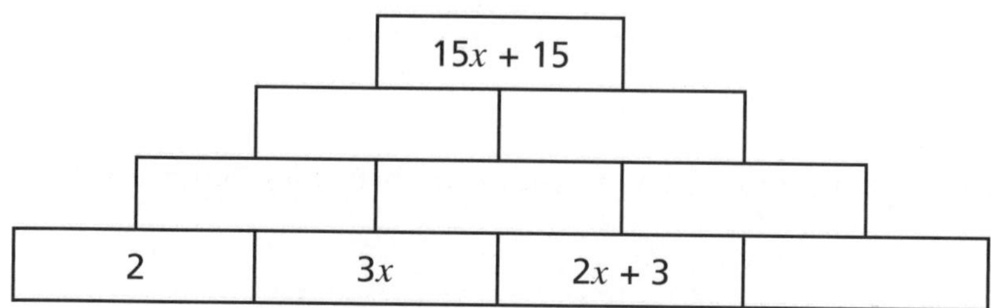

[2]

3 **a)** Complete this algebraic multiplication table.

×	$2x$	1
$3x$		
5	$10x$	

[2]

b) Use your answer to part a) to multiply out and simplify $3x(2x + 1) + 5(2x + 1)$

.... [1]

Total Marks .... / 11

	.... / 44
	.... / 17
	.... / 11

How do you feel about these skills?

PS MR FS

Green = Got it!
Orange = Nearly there
Red = Needs practice

Fractions

Video Solution Question 1

1 Five pizzas are each cut into six equal pieces.

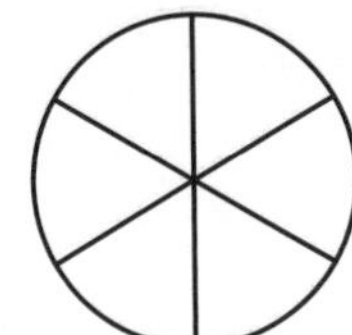 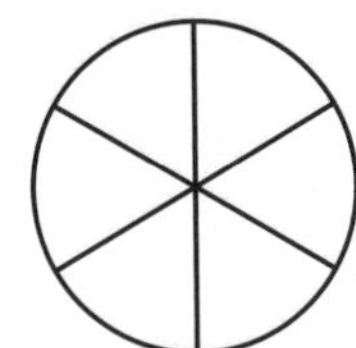 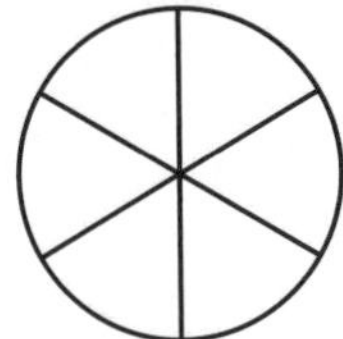 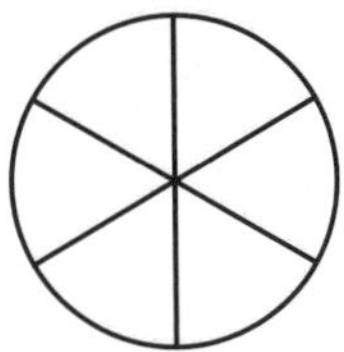 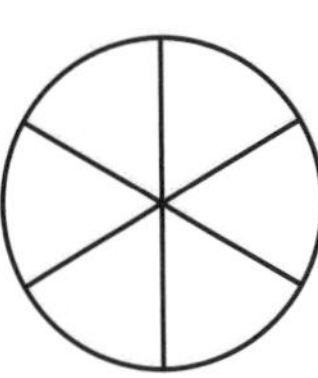

The five pizzas are shared equally between six people.

What fraction of a pizza does each person get?

.... [1]

2 Write each fraction in its simplest form.

a) $\frac{4}{6}$ = ... b) $\frac{12}{20}$ = ... c) $\frac{9}{9}$ = ...

d) $\frac{86}{100}$ = ... e) $\frac{15}{35}$ = ... f) $\frac{54}{72}$ = ... [6]

3 Work out:

a) $4 \times \frac{1}{5}$ .... b) $\frac{1}{6} \times 2$ .... c) $\frac{3}{4} \times 3$ ....

d) $\frac{1}{4} \times \frac{1}{7}$ .... e) $\frac{1}{3} \times \frac{1}{8}$ .... f) $\frac{2}{3} \times \frac{1}{5}$ ....

g) $\frac{1}{4} \times \frac{5}{6}$ .... h) $\frac{3}{5} \times \frac{2}{7}$ .... i) $\frac{5}{8} \times \frac{3}{10}$ .... [9]

4 Work out:

a) $1 - \frac{2}{5}$ .... b) $3 - \frac{5}{6}$ .... c) $\frac{7}{9} - \frac{5}{9}$ ....

d) $\frac{1}{4} - \frac{1}{8}$ .... e) $\frac{1}{3} + \frac{1}{6}$ .... f) $\frac{1}{3} + \frac{1}{4}$ ....

g) $\frac{1}{4} - \frac{1}{6}$ .... h) $\frac{2}{5} + \frac{1}{4}$ .... i) $\frac{3}{8} + \frac{2}{5}$ .... [9]

5 Write each improper fraction as a mixed number.

a) $\frac{9}{8}$ = ... b) $\frac{17}{4}$ = ... c) $\frac{20}{3}$ = ... [3]

Fractions

Video Solution Question 4

6 Write each mixed number as an improper fraction.

a) $1\frac{1}{4}$ = ... b) $3\frac{1}{5}$ = ... c) $5\frac{3}{7}$ = ... [3]

7 Work out:

a) $\frac{1}{4} \div 3$ .... b) $\frac{4}{5} \div 2$ .... c) $\frac{2}{3} \div 6$ .... [3]

8 Convert each decimal to a fraction in its lowest terms.

a) 0.73 = ... b) 0.284 = ... c) 0.36 = ... [3]

PS 9 There are 340 people at a cinema. One-quarter of these are children.

How many children are at the cinema?

.... [1]

Total Marks .... / 38

1 Work out:

a) $\frac{1}{5} \div \frac{1}{2}$ .... b) $\frac{1}{4} \div \frac{1}{3}$ .... c) $\frac{1}{3} \div \frac{2}{5}$ ....

d) $\frac{1}{10} \div \frac{2}{5}$ .... e) $\frac{5}{6} \div \frac{7}{8}$ .... f) $\frac{4}{9} \div \frac{2}{3}$ .... [6]

2 Convert each fraction to a decimal.

a) $\frac{7}{10}$ = ... b) $\frac{23}{100}$ = ... c) $\frac{409}{1000}$ = ...

d) $\frac{1}{4}$ = ... e) $\frac{1}{20}$ = ... f) $\frac{13}{25}$ = ...

g) $\frac{5}{8}$ = ... h) $\frac{3}{7}$ = ... i) $\frac{2}{9}$ = ... [9]

PS 3 Write these fractions in order, starting with the smallest:

$\frac{2}{9}$ $\frac{11}{12}$ $\frac{1}{2}$ $\frac{3}{7}$ $\frac{1}{6}$ $\frac{7}{11}$

.... [2]

(PS) **4** Write these in order, starting with the smallest:

$0.8 \quad \frac{2}{9} \quad \frac{3}{4} \quad 0.35 \quad \frac{5}{6} \quad \frac{1}{3}$

.... [2]

5 Work out:

a) $3 \div \frac{1}{2}$ .... b) $15 \div \frac{1}{3}$ .... c) $8 \div \frac{2}{5}$ .... [3]

(PS) **6** There are 90 passengers on a train. Two-fifths of the passengers have a rail card.

How many passengers have a rail card?

.... [1]

(MR) **7** Write the correct sign (<, > or =) in each space.

a) $\frac{1}{3} \times 6$ .... $\frac{1}{3}$ b) $\frac{1}{3} \times \frac{1}{3}$ .... $\frac{1}{3}$ c) $\frac{1}{3} \times 3$ 1

d) $\frac{1}{6} \times \frac{1}{3}$ .... 2 e) $\frac{1}{6} \div \frac{1}{3}$ .... $\frac{1}{2}$ f) $\frac{2}{3} \div \frac{1}{6}$ .... 3 [6]

8 A farmer has 32 white sheep and 18 black sheep.

What fraction of the sheep are black? Give your answer in its simplest form.

.... [2]

9 Work out:

a) $2\frac{1}{2} + \frac{2}{5}$ .... [1]

b) $5\frac{2}{3} - \frac{7}{8}$ .... [1]

c) $3\frac{2}{5} - 2\frac{1}{4}$ .... [1]

Total Marks .... / 34

1 Work out:

a) $1\frac{1}{4} \times \frac{2}{3}$ .... [1]

b) $3\frac{2}{5} \div \frac{5}{6}$ .... [1]

c) $4\frac{1}{5} \div 1\frac{3}{4}$ .... [1]

Fractions

MR **2** Work out the missing value. 

$$2\frac{1}{3} \times \text{..........} = 1$$ [1]

PS **3** Two-thirds of the children in a class sing in the choir.
Of those children, one-quarter play guitar.

What fraction of the children in the class sing in the choir and play guitar?

.... [1]

MR **4** Use the multiplication fact $\frac{2}{13} \times 351 = 54$ to work out: 

a) $\frac{1}{13} \times 351$ .... [1]

b) $\frac{4}{13} \times 351$ .... [1]

c) $\frac{4}{26} \times 351$ .... [1]

MR **5** What value is at the midpoint of this number line?

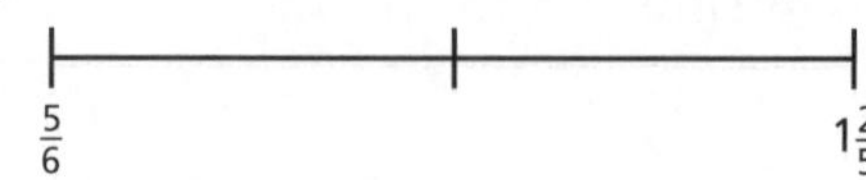

.... [1]

PS **6** Marie ate five-eighths of the sweets in a bag. 9 sweets were left.

How many sweets were in the bag to start with?

.... [1]

PS **7** Write these in order, starting with the lowest value:

$-0.6 \quad \frac{3}{5} \quad -1\frac{1}{4} \quad 0.7 \quad -\frac{2}{3}$

.... [2]

Total Marks .... / 12

	.... / 38
	.... / 34
	.... / 12

How do you feel about these skills?

Green = Got it!
Orange = Nearly there
Red = Needs practice

Video Solution Question 3

1 Draw lines to join each quadrilateral to its correct name.

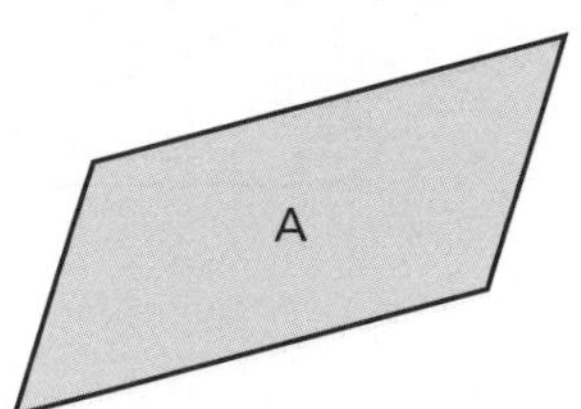

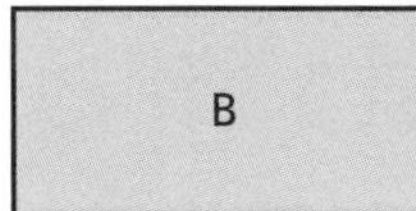

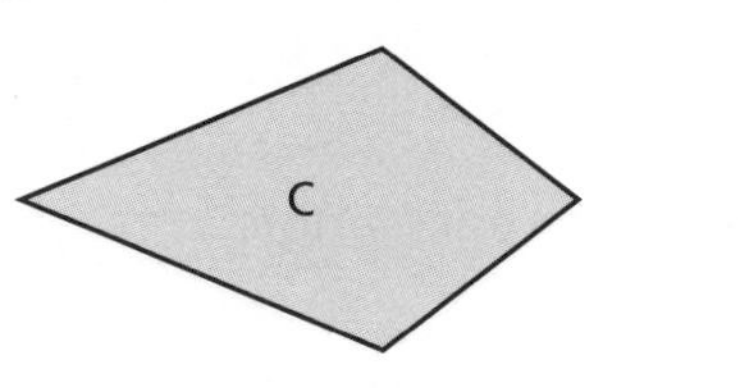

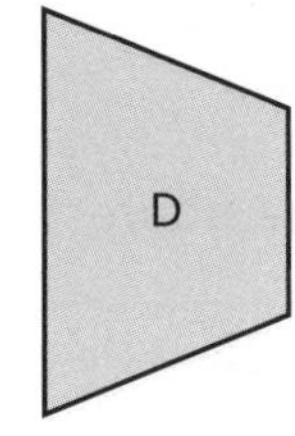

Kite

Rhombus

Parallelogram

Trapezium

Rectangle

[4]

2 Write down the sizes of the reflex angles in this diagram.

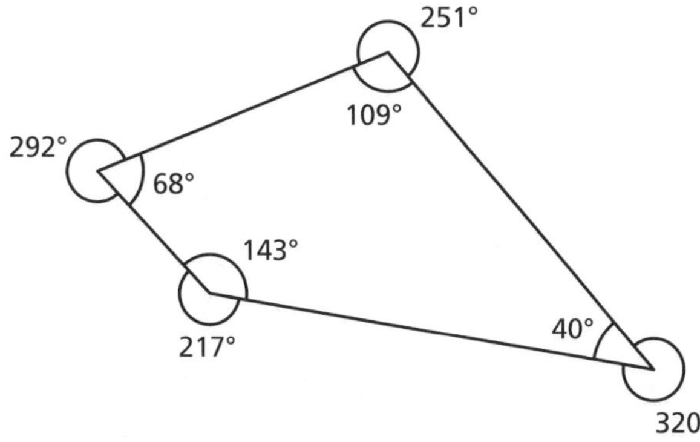

.... [1]

MR 3 What type of triangle am I?

a) All three of my angles are equal .... [1]

b) Exactly two of my angles are equal .... [1]

c) One of my angles is 90° .... [1]

d) My angles are all different and none of them is 90° .... [1]

4 Find the sizes of the lettered angles.

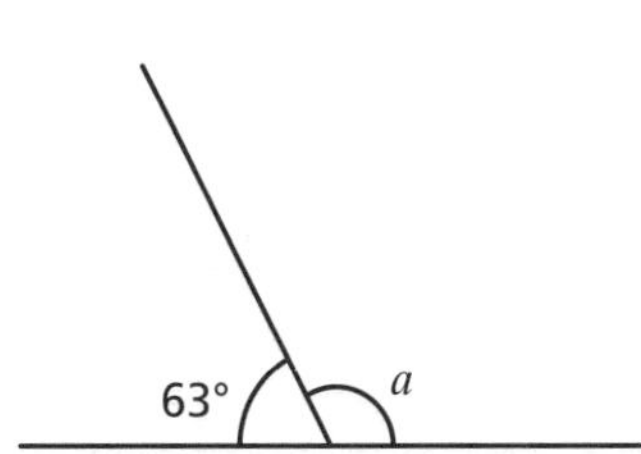

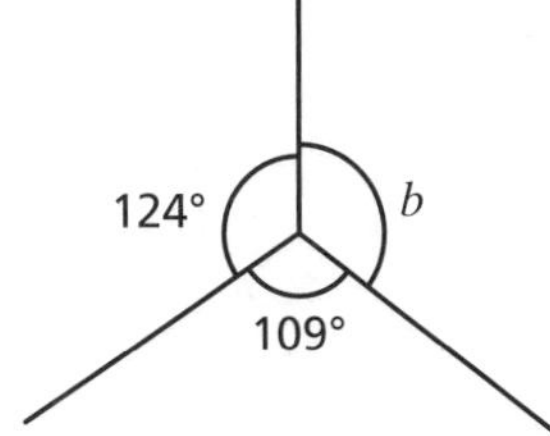

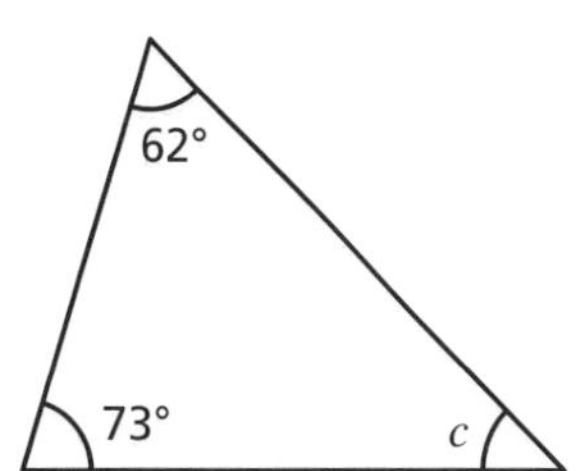

$a =$ .... ° $b =$ .... ° $c =$ .... ° [3]

Video Solution Question 4

MR **5** Dougal works out the value of angle x.
He says that x equals 23°.

Explain clearly why Dougal is **not** correct.

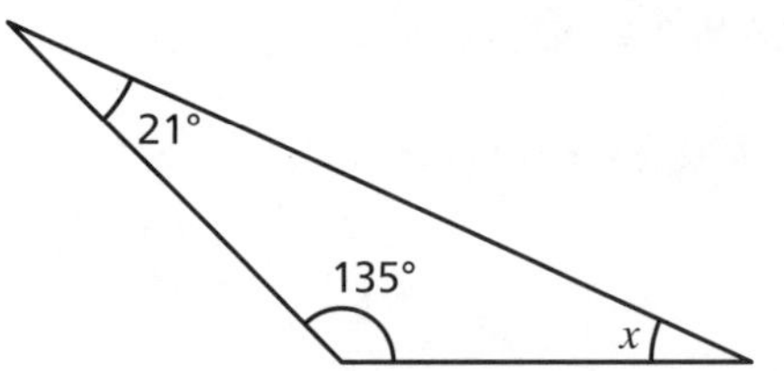

[2]

6 Use a protractor to measure these angles to the nearest degree. For each angle, write down if it is acute, obtuse or reflex.

a)

b)

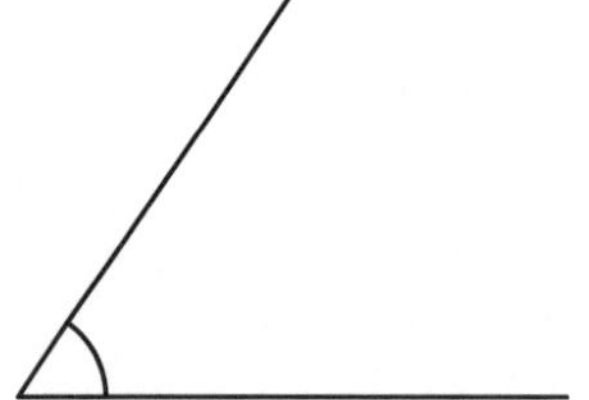

c)

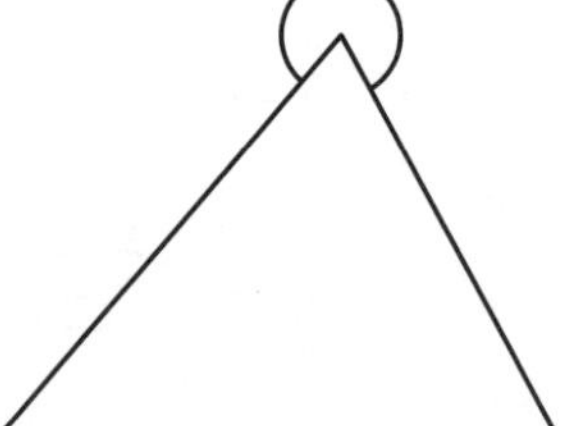

[6]

Total Marks .... / 20

PS **1** Work out the size of each lettered angle.

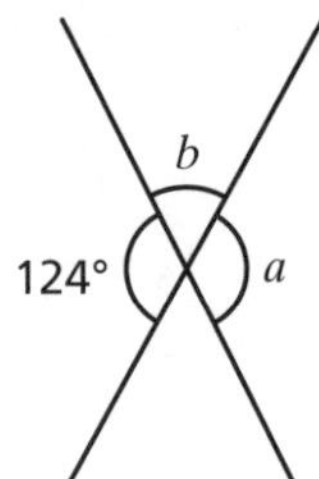

$a =$ ....°

$b =$ ....°

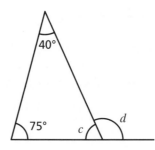

$c =$ ....°

$d =$ ....°

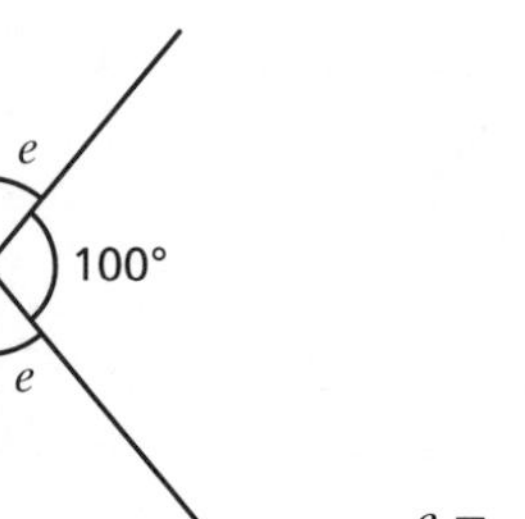

$e =$ ....°

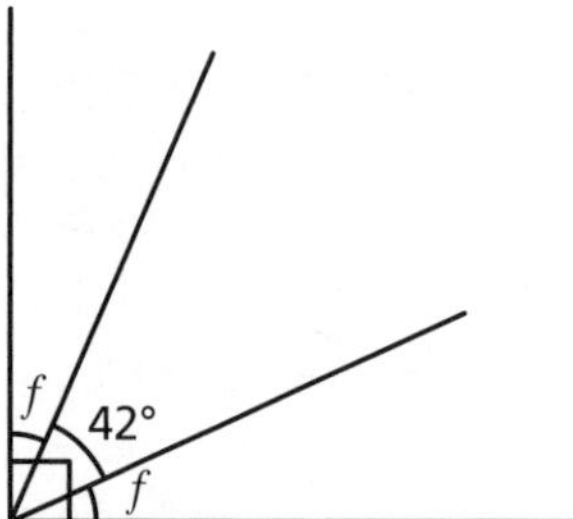

$f =$ ....°

[6]

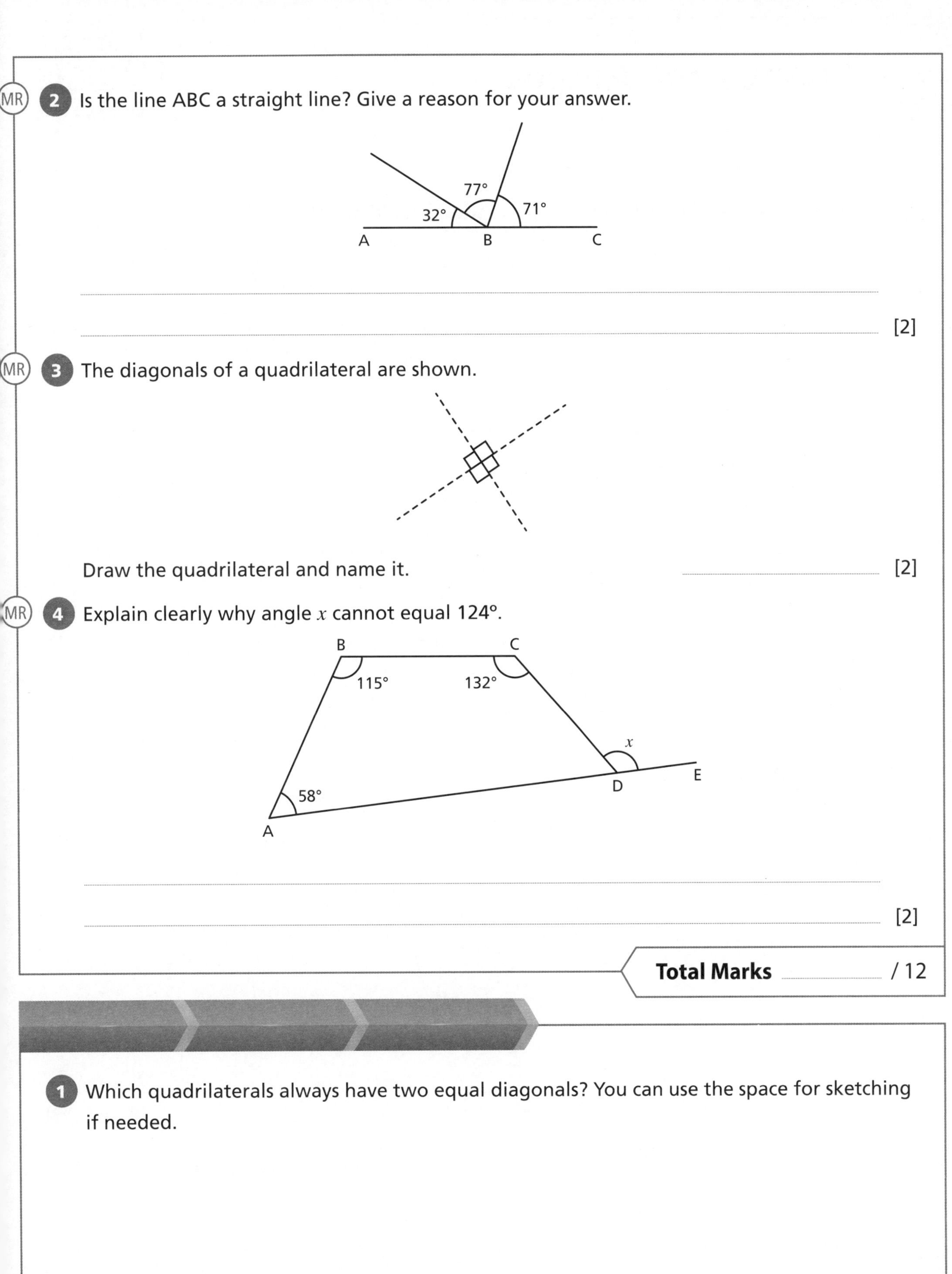

MR **2** Is the line ABC a straight line? Give a reason for your answer.

[2]

MR **3** The diagonals of a quadrilateral are shown.

Draw the quadrilateral and name it. [2]

MR **4** Explain clearly why angle x cannot equal 124°.

[2]

Total Marks / 12

1 Which quadrilaterals always have two equal diagonals? You can use the space for sketching if needed.

[2]

Shapes and Angles

PS **2** Work out the size of each lettered angle in these quadrilaterals.

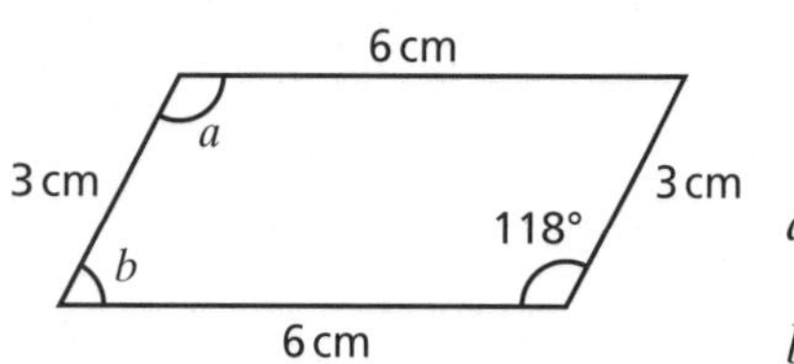

$a =$ .... °

$b =$ .... °

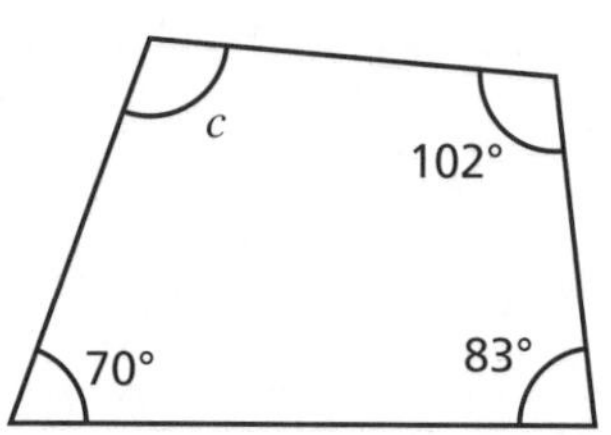

$c =$ .... °

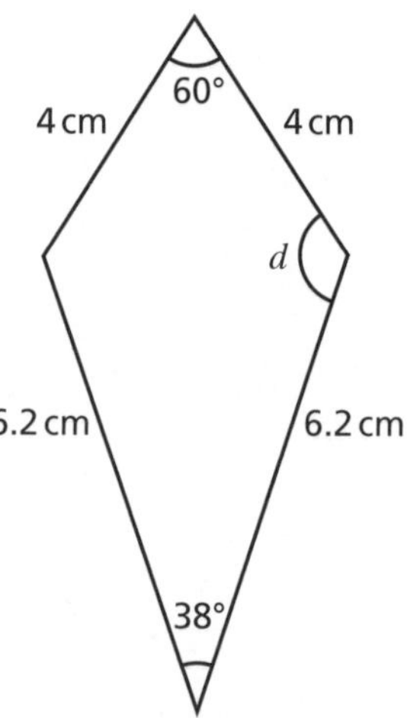

$d =$ .... °

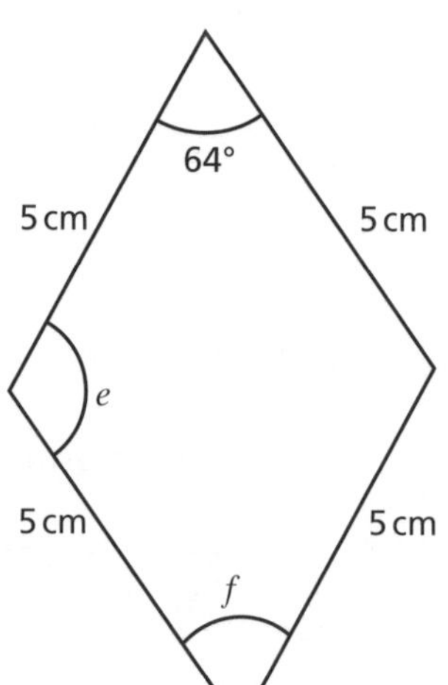

$e =$ .... °

$f =$ .... ° [6]

PS **3** Work out the size of each lettered angle.

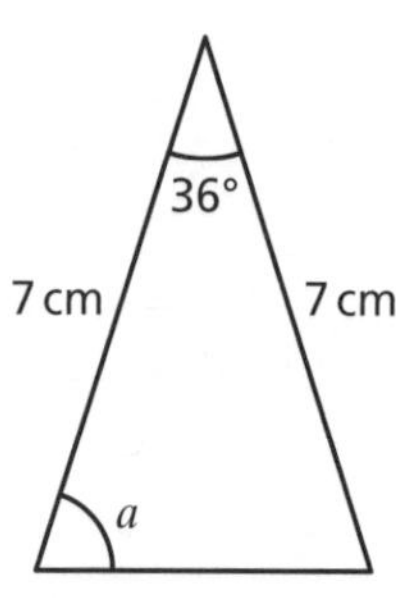

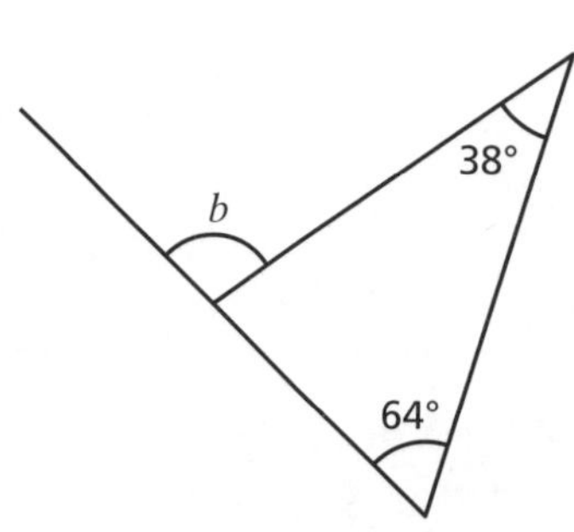

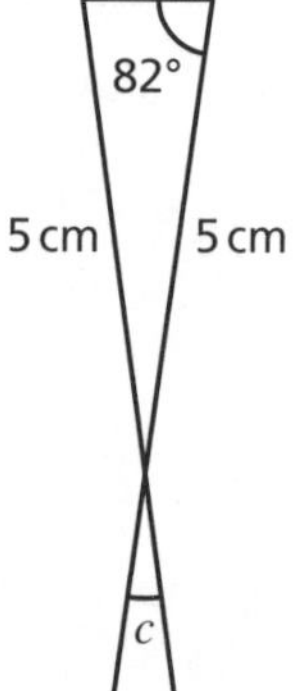

$a =$ .... ° $b =$ .... ° $c =$ .... ° [3]

Total Marks .... / 11

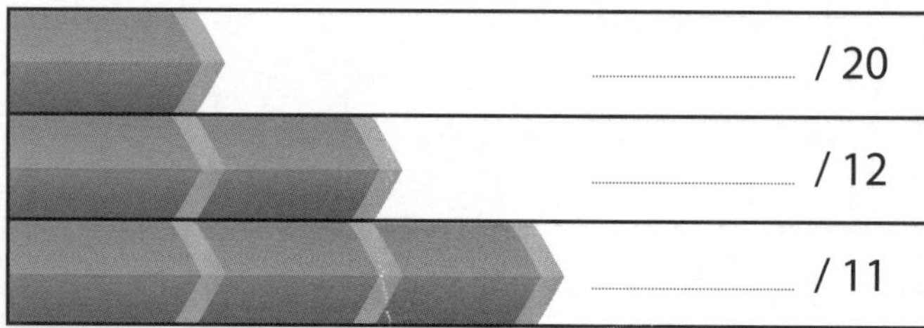

	.... / 20
	.... / 12
	.... / 11

How do you feel about these skills?

Green = Got it!
Orange = Nearly there
Red = Needs practice

Coordinates and Graphs

Video Solution Question 1

1 For each part, plot the points on the grid. Join the points in order to make a quadrilateral. Name the quadrilateral.

Draw the quadrilaterals in parts a) and b) on the first grid and the quadrilaterals in parts c) and d) on the second grid.

a) (–6, 1), (–4, 1), (–4, –1), (–6, –1)

.... [2]

b) (3, 4), (5, 2), (3, –4), (1, 2)

.... [2]

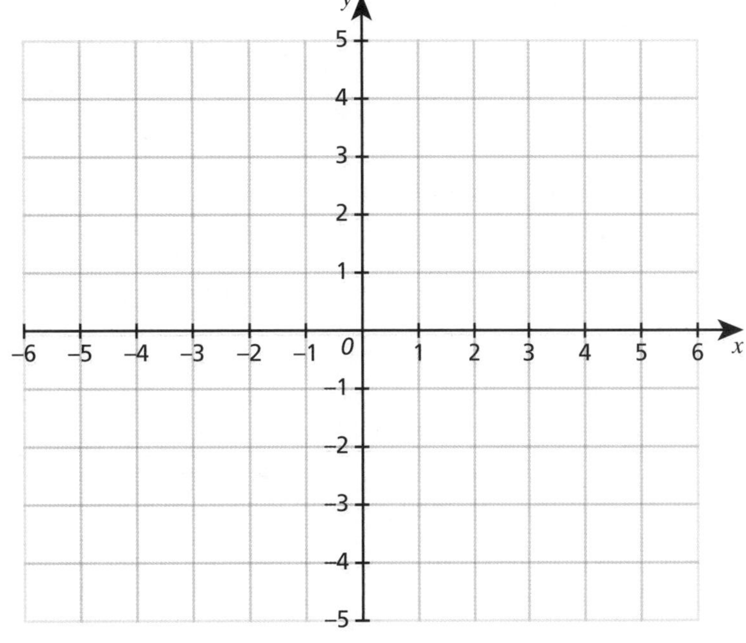

c) (–3, –1), (–1, –1), (0, –4), (–5, –4)

.... [2]

d) (–5, 2), (–1, 2), (–1, 4), (–5, 4)

.... [2]

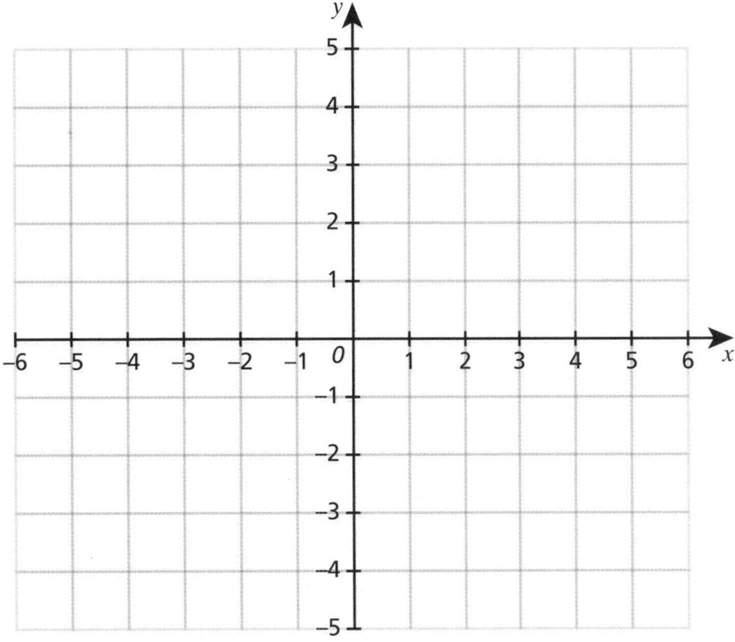

Video Solution Question 1

PS **2** (–5, –2), (–1, 3) and (5, 3) are the coordinates of three points of a parallelogram.

Work out the coordinates of the fourth point.

(........., ...) [2]

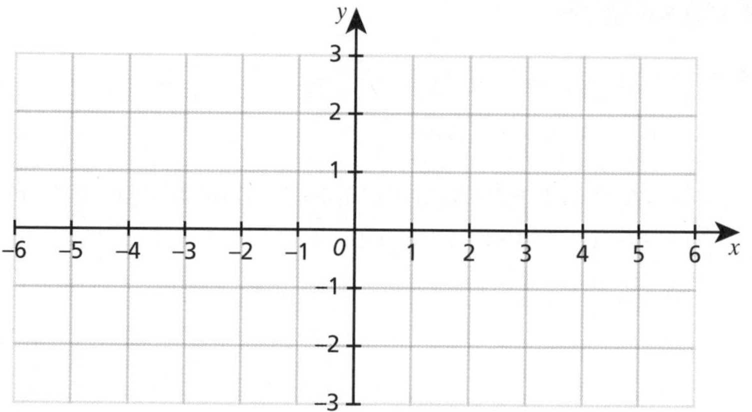

3 Write down the equations of each line.

A ....

B ....

C ....

D ....

E .... [5]

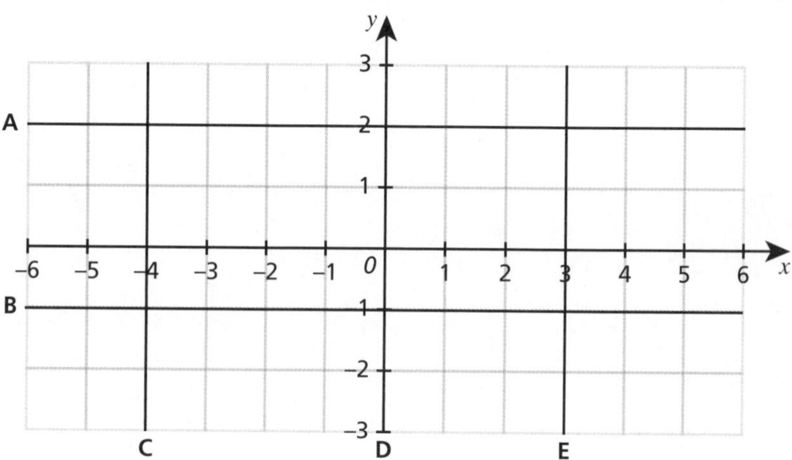

4 Look at the coordinate grid. Write down the letters that are on each line.

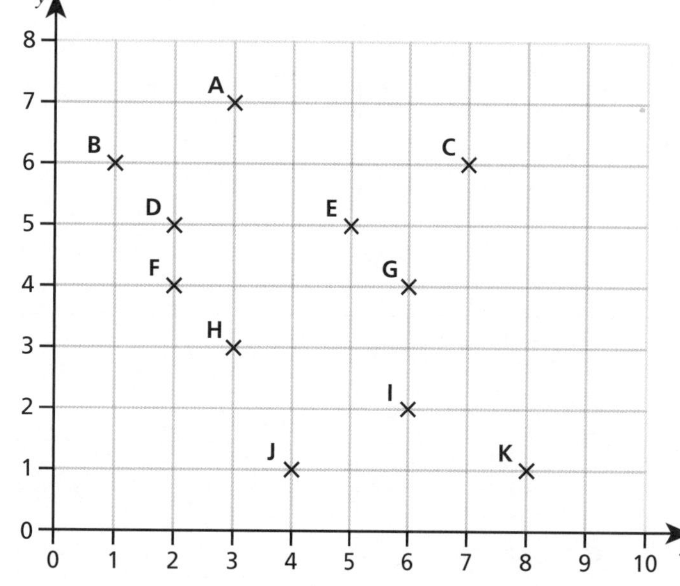

a) $x = 2$ .... [1]

b) $y = 4$ .... [1]

c) $x = 5$ .... [1]

d) $y = 7$ .... [1]

e) $x = 6$ .... [1]

f) $y = 6$ .... [1]

Total Marks .... / 21

1 The diagram shows five straight lines.

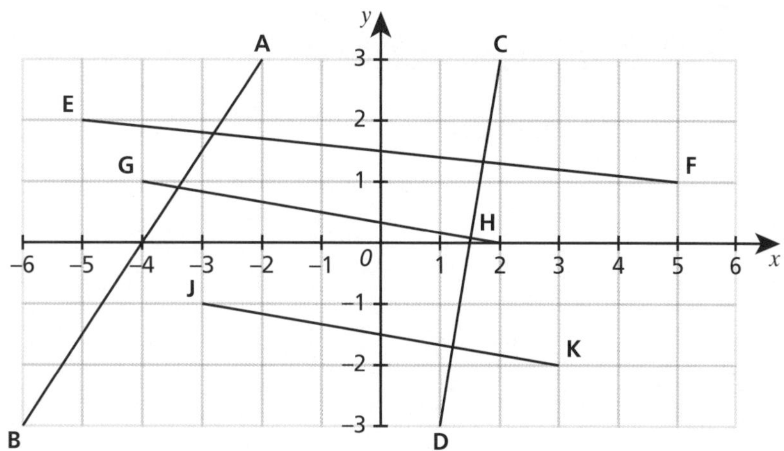

a) Which line is parallel to line GH? .... [1]

b) Which line is perpendicular to line GH? .... [1]

2 **a)** Complete the table of values for the equation $y = x$

x	0	2	4
y			

[1]

b) Complete the table of values for the equation $y = x + 2$

x	0	2	4
y			

[1]

c) Complete the table of values for the equation $y = 2x$

x	0	2	4
y			

[1]

d) On the grid, draw and label the graphs of $y = x$, $y = x + 2$ and $y = 2x$

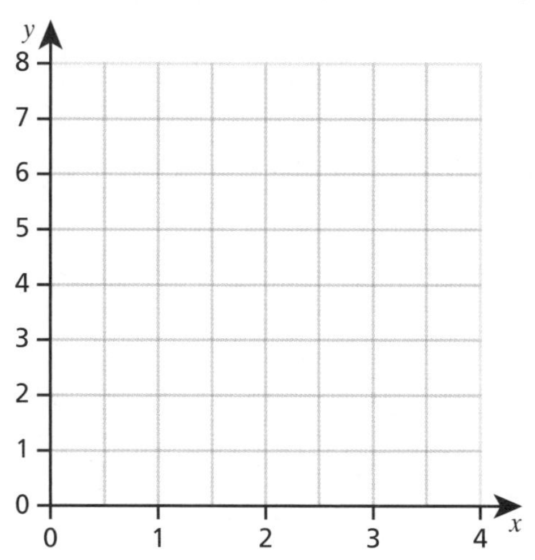

[3]

Total Marks .... / 8

Video Solution Question 3

1 Use the graph to answer the questions.

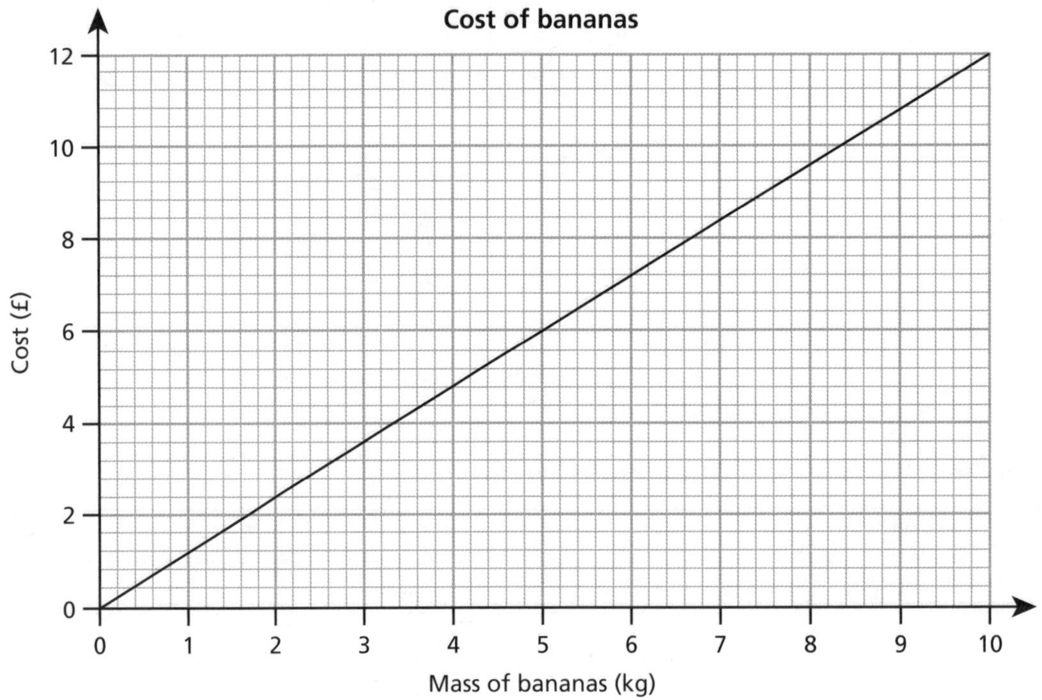

a) Work out the cost of 5 kg of bananas.

£ .... [1]

b) Work out the cost of 20 kg of bananas.

£ .... [1]

c) What mass of bananas can be bought for £3?

.... kg [1]

FS **2** The exchange rate between the pound (£) and the euro (€) is €1 = £0.90

a) Complete the table to show how many pounds you would get for the given number of euros.

Euros (€)	1	10	20	30
Pounds (£)	0.90			

[2]

b) Draw the conversion graph.

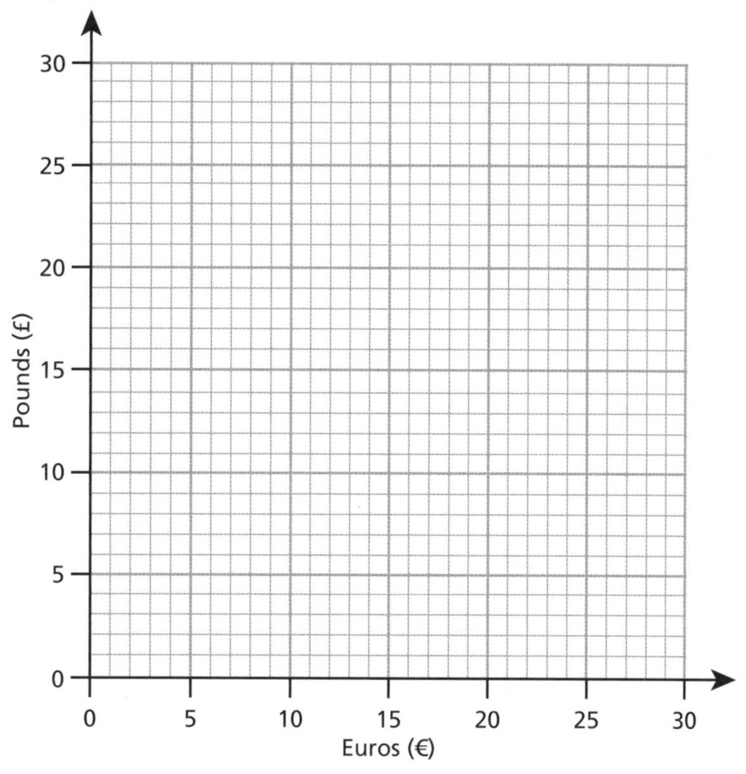

[2]

c) Use the graph to convert €25 to pounds. £ .... [1]

d) Without carrying out the calculation, explain how you can convert £1500 to euros using the graph.

....

.... [1]

MR **3** Here are some coordinates. (–4, –1), (–1, 2), (4, 7)

Which of the following is the equation of the line passing through all three coordinates? Circle your answer.

A $y = 4x$ **B** $y = x + 3$ **C** $y = x - 3$ **D** $y = 3x$ [1]

Total Marks .... / 10

....	/ 21
....	/ 8
....	/ 10

How do you feel about these skills?

PS MR FS

Green = Got it!
Orange = Nearly there
Red = Needs practice

Percentages

Video Solution Question 6

1 Write the percentage shaded in each grid.

a) 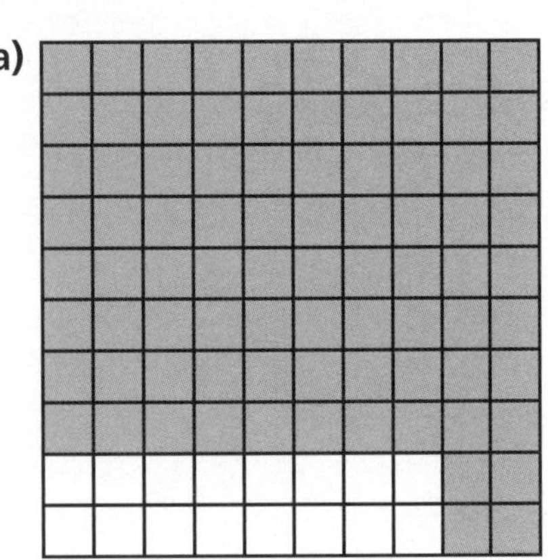

b) 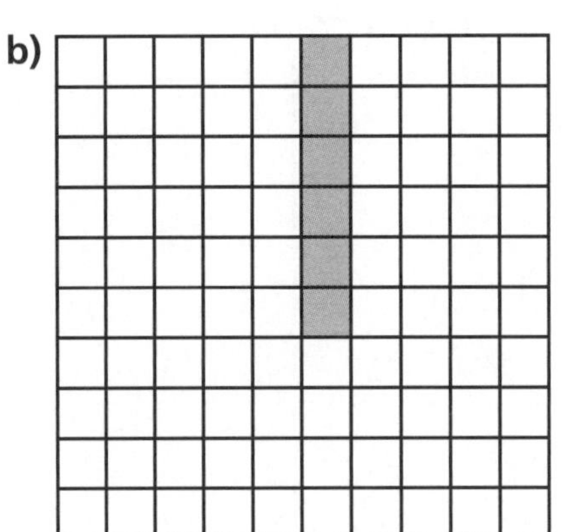

.... % .... % [2]

2 Write each percentage as a fraction in its simplest form.

a) 50% = ... b) 10% = ... c) 25% = ...

d) 20% = ... e) 75% = ... f) 80% = ...

g) 46% = ... h) 9% = ... i) 8% = ... [9]

3 Write each percentage as a decimal.

a) 35% = ... b) 42% = ... c) 60% = ...

d) 2% = ... e) 37.5% = ... f) 2.5% = ... [6]

4 Write each decimal as a percentage.

a) 0.72 = ... % b) 0.15 = ... % c) 0.07 = ... %

d) 0.245 = ... % e) 1.75 = ... % f) 0.004 = ... % [6]

PS 5 Write these in order, starting with the smallest:

$\frac{2}{5}$ 0.8 20% $\frac{1}{2}$ 65%

.... [2]

6 Work out:

a) 10% of £80 £........ b) 50% of 4 kg .... kg

c) 25% of 10 m .... m d) 20% of 30 cm .... cm

e) 10% of 30p .... p f) 75% of 12 km .... km [6]

Total Marks .... / 31

(FS) **1** Calculate:

a) 10% of £36 £ .... [1]

b) 5% of £36 £ .... [1]

c) 15% of £36 £ .... [1]

d) 7% of £36 £ .... [1]

(MR) **2** Complete these fraction-to-percentage conversions.

a) $\frac{13}{50} = \frac{\square}{100} =$ .... %

b) $\frac{88}{200} = \frac{\square}{100} =$ .... %

c) $\frac{9}{25} = \frac{\square}{100} =$ .... %

d) $\frac{11}{20} = \frac{\square}{100} =$ .... % [8]

(PS) **3** Katya scored $\frac{47}{50}$ in a test.

What was her score as a percentage?

.... % [1]

(PS) **4** Some children were asked to choose their favourite sport. The bar chart shows the results.

What percentage of children chose each of the following sports?

a) Tennis

.... %

b) Football

.... %

c) Swimming or hockey

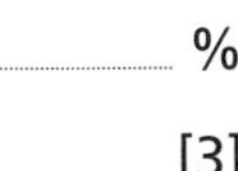

.... %

[3]

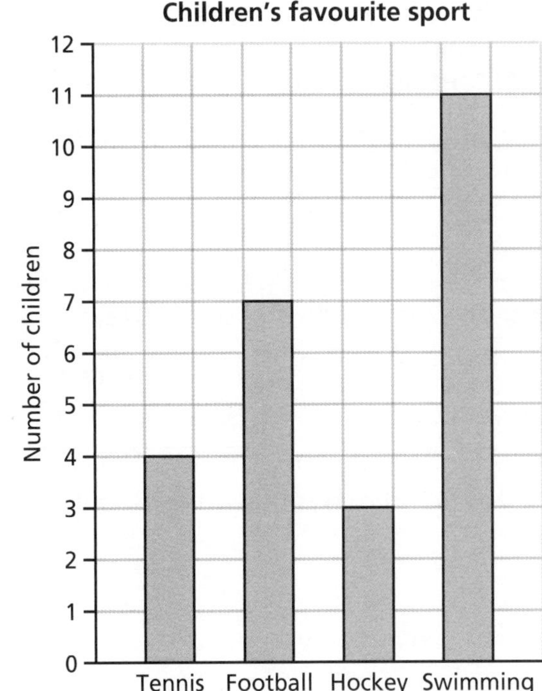

(FS) **5** Class 7B raised £510 in a raffle.

They gave 30% of this amount to a wildlife charity.

How much did they give to the wildlife charity?

£ .... [1]

Total Marks .... / 17

Percentages

Video Solution Question 2

MR **1** Write the correct symbol (<, = or >) in each space.

a) 20% of 17 cm .... 25% of 12 cm [1]

b) 15% of 90 kg .... 20% of 80 kg [1]

c) 60% of £50 .... 40% of £75 [1]

PS MR **2** Here are Tom's marks in three tests.

Test A	Test B	Test C
$\frac{17}{20}$	$\frac{39}{50}$	$\frac{21}{25}$

In which test did Tom score:

a) the highest percentage? .... [1]

b) the lowest percentage? .... [1]

FS **3** A T-shirt costs £22. Dan buys the T-shirt at a 30% discount.

How much money does he save?

£ .... [1]

FS **4** The same style and size of trainers are for sale on two different websites.

Website X	**Website Y**
£90 with 20% off	£100 with $\frac{1}{4}$ off

a) Which website would you buy the trainers from?

.... [1]

b) Explain why. ....

.... [1]

Total Marks .... / 8

	.... / 31
	.... / 17
	.... / 8

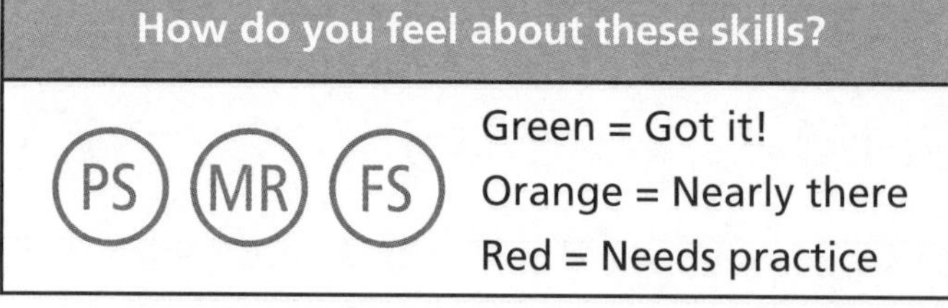

How do you feel about these skills?
PS
MR
FS
Green = Got it!
Orange = Nearly there
Red = Needs practice

Symmetry and Transformations

Video Solution Question 1

1 Draw all possible lines of symmetry (if any) on each of these shapes.

 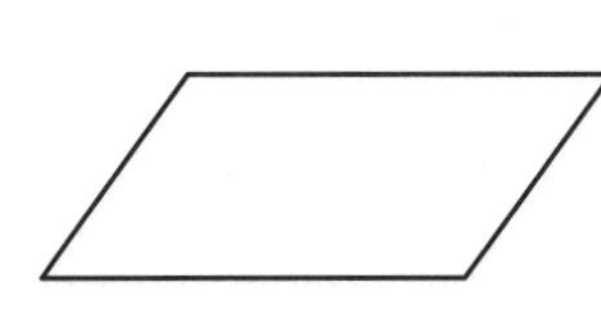  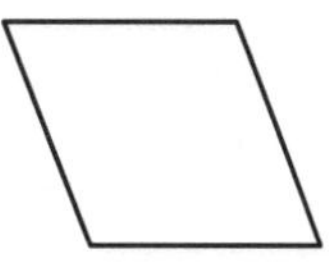 

[5]

2 The two letters shown are reflected in the dashed line.

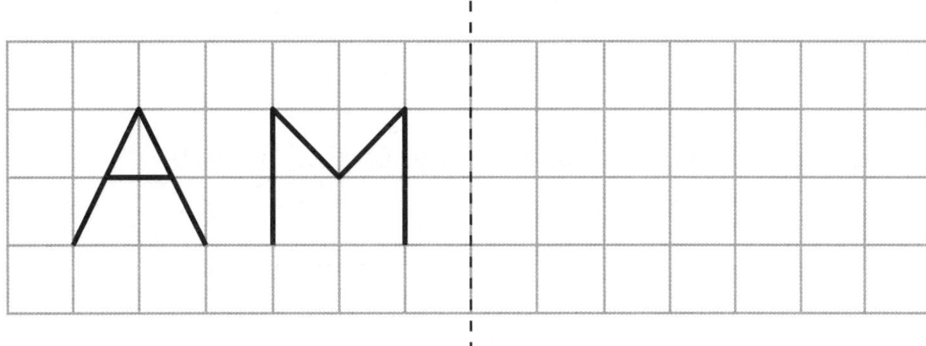

What word will they spell? .... [1]

MR 3 Reflect this parallelogram in the y-axis.

Draw the image on the coordinate grid. [2]

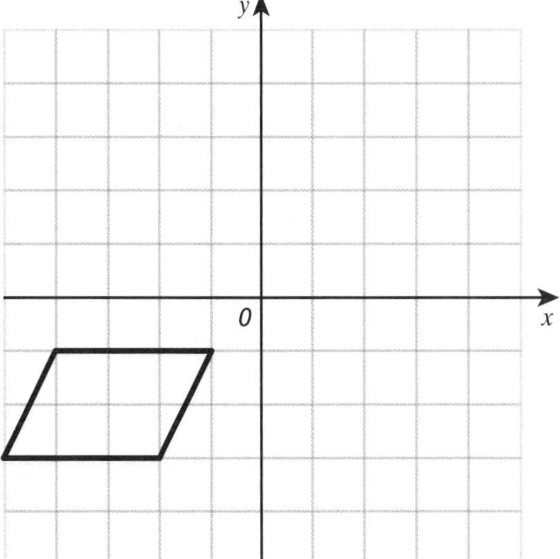

4 An object is rotated 90° clockwise to produce an image.

How many degrees anti-clockwise could the original object be rotated to produce the same image? .... ° [1]

Total Marks .... / 9

Symmetry and Transformations

Video Solution Question 2

MR **1** Shade the minimum number of squares needed in this diagram so that the dashed line is a line of symmetry.

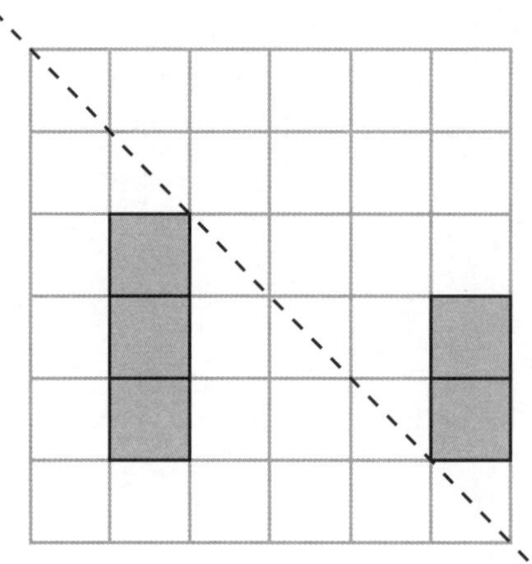

[2]

2 Here is a shape drawn on a grid with two points, B and C, marked.

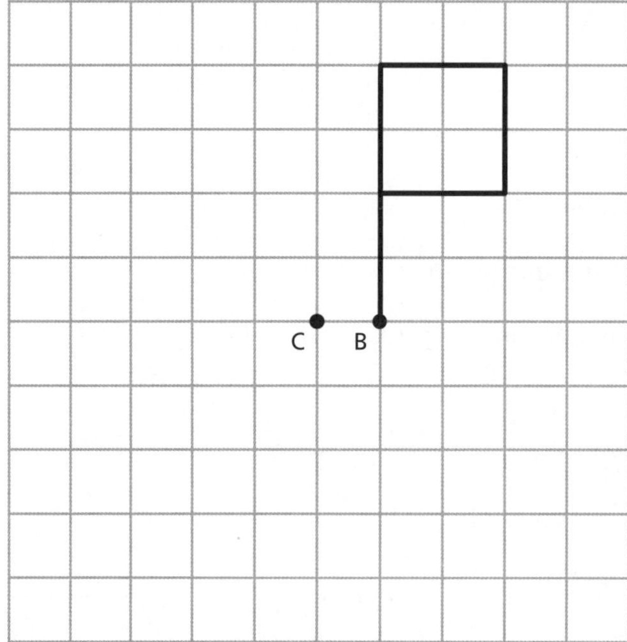

a) Draw the shape after a rotation of 180° about the point B. [2]

b) Draw the shape after a rotation of 90° anti-clockwise about the point C. [2]

MR **3** Triangle P is shown on the coordinate grid.

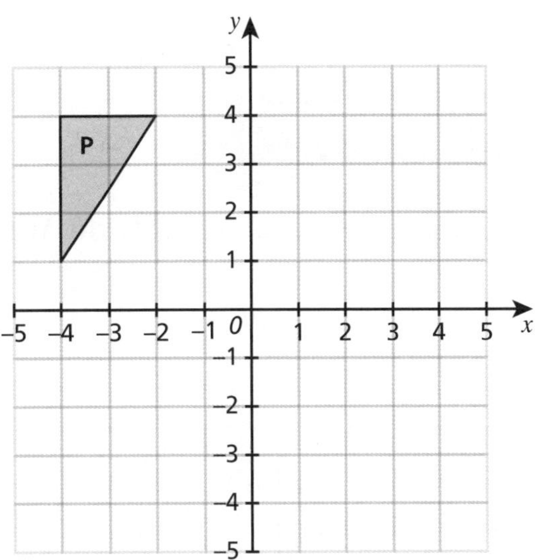

a) Reflect triangle P in the x-axis.

Label the image Q. [2]

b) In which line must triangle Q be reflected to end up back in triangle P's starting position?

.... [1]

4 What two pieces of information are needed to fully describe the enlargement of an object?

.... and .... [2]

5 Shapes A, B, C, D and E are shown on the coordinate grid.

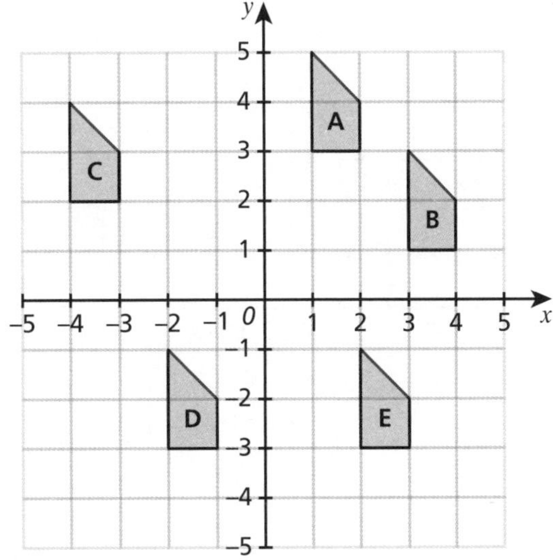

Describe the following translations.

a) A ➝ B .... [1]

b) A ➝ C .... [1]

c) D ➝ B .... [1]

d) E ➝ D .... [1]

Total Marks .... / 15

Video Solution Question 5

(MR) **1** Two triangles, P and Q, are shown on the coordinate grid. Triangle Q is an enlargement of triangle P.

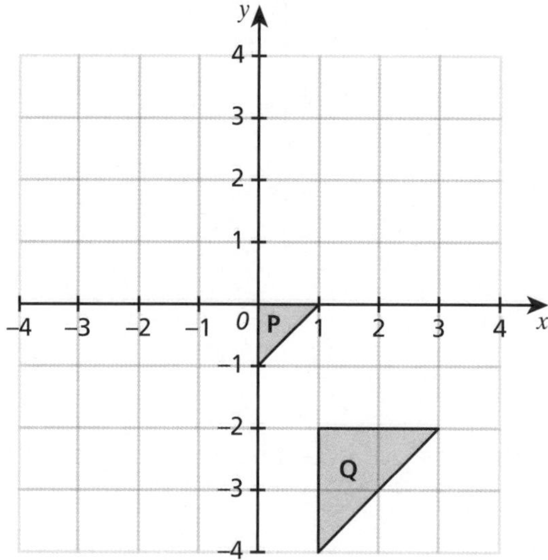

a) What is the scale factor of enlargement from triangle P to triangle Q? .... [1]

b) What is the centre of enlargement? .... [1]

2 Shape P is shown on the coordinate grid.

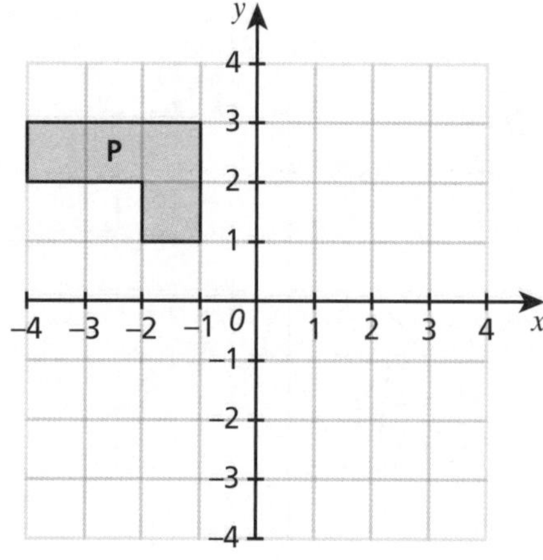

a) Rotate shape P 90° clockwise about (0, 0). Label the image Q. [2]

b) Reflect Q in the x-axis. Label the image R. [2]

(MR) **3** A shape is translated by 2 units to the left and 6 units up.

Describe the translation that takes the image back to the original shape's position.

.... [1]

PS **4** Shape A is shown on the coordinate grid.

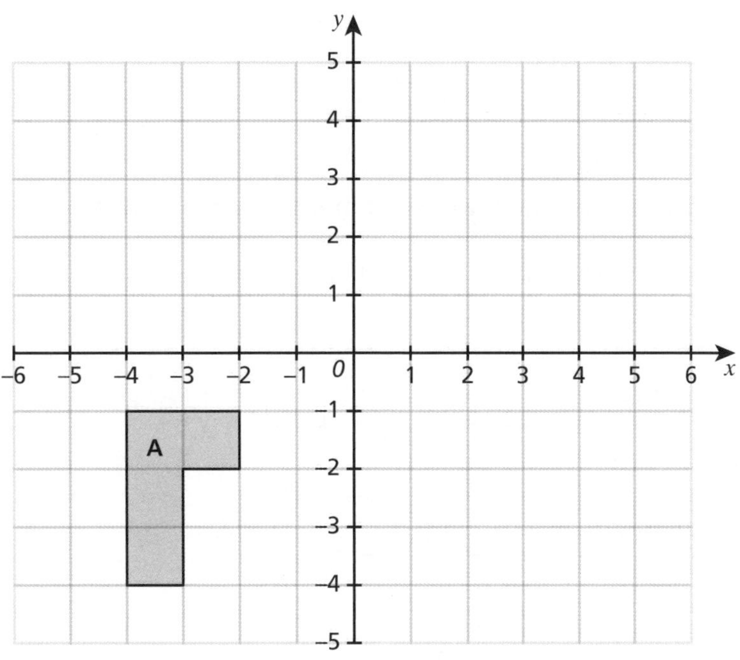

a) Rotate shape A 180° about (0, 0). Label the image B. [2]

b) Rotate shape B 180° about (4, 1). Label the image C. [2]

c) Describe the translation that takes A to C.

.... [1]

PS **5** Rectangle A is shown on the coordinate grid.

a) Enlarge rectangle A by scale factor 3 about the centre of enlargement (0, 0). Label the image B. [2]

b) Enlarge rectangle A by scale factor 3 about the centre of enlargement (1, 2). Label the image C. [2]

c) Describe the translation of rectangle B to rectangle C.

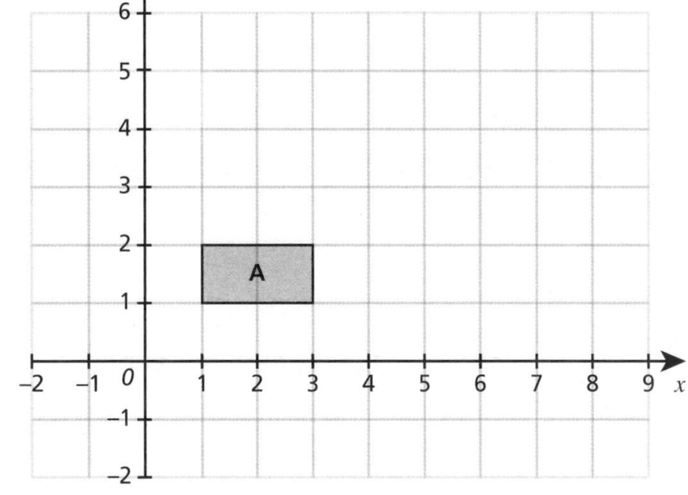

.... [1]

Total Marks .... / 17

	.... / 9
	.... / 15
	.... / 17

How do you feel about these skills?

Green = Got it!
Orange = Nearly there
Red = Needs practice

Equations

Video Solution Question 4

1 Decide whether each of the following statements is **true** or **false**.

a) 2 is the missing value in $3 \times \square + 7 = 13$

.... [1]

b) 6 is the missing value in $2 + \square \times 3 = 14 + \square$

.... [1]

c) 9 is the missing value in $40 - \square \times 3 = \square + 2 \times 2$

.... [1]

d) 4 is the missing value in $12 \div \square + 2 = 2$

.... [1]

FS 2 I have 20p and 5p coins in a purse. The total amount of these coins is 55p.

a) Write this as a symbol sentence and find **two** possible numbers of each coin.

Symbol sentence: ....

Two possible numbers of each coin: .... [3]

b) Work out the smallest possible number of coins in my purse.

.... [1]

3 Fill in the missing values in each equation.

a) $\square + 6 = 13$ **b)** $\square - 4 = 15$ **c)** $\square + 9 = 5$

d) $\square - 6 = -2$ **e)** $4 \times \square = 16$ **f)** $\square \div 5 = 9$ [6]

(MR) **4** Write each of the following bar models as equations in **three** different ways.

The first one has been done for you.

a)

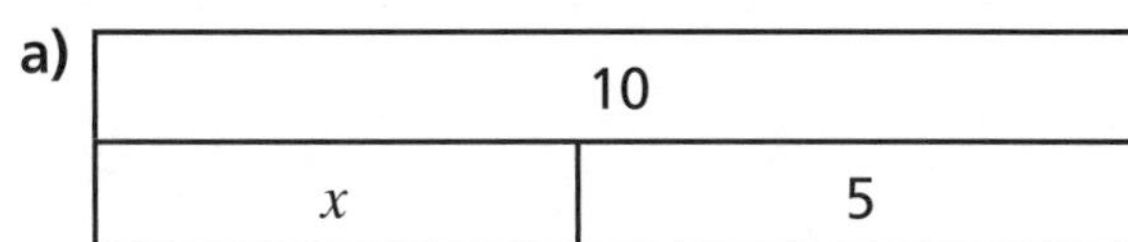

Answer: $x + 5 = 10$ $10 - x = 5$ $10 - 5 = x$

b)

12	
y	3

.... [1]

c)

b	12
15	

.... [1]

d)

20			
a	a	a	8

.... [1]

e) For parts a) to d), work out the values of x, y, b and a.

$x =$ ....

$y =$ ....

$b =$ ....

$a =$ .... [4]

(MR) **5** In this number wall, the number of each brick is the sum of the numbers in the two bricks below it.

Work out the values of a, b and c.

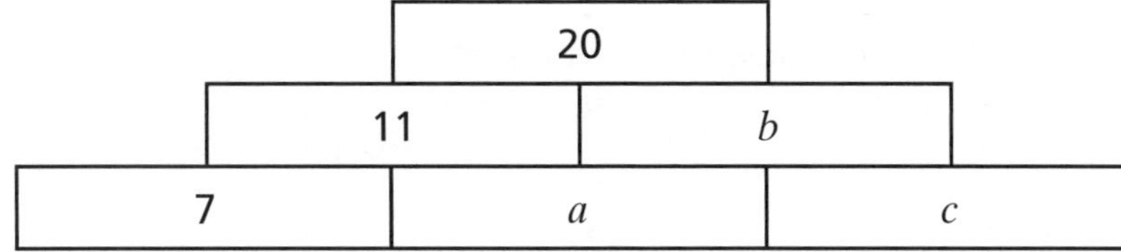

$a =$ ....

$b =$ ....

$c =$ .... [3]

Equations

Video Solution Question 1

MR **6** I think of a number, x. I multiply it by 5. I then add 4.

a) Write down an expression to show what I did.

.... [1]

b) Work out the value of x if the answer is 24.

$x =$ .... [2]

c) Work out the value of x if the answer is 39.

$x =$ .... [2]

MR **7** I think of a number. I add 6. I then multiply by 3. My answer is 33.

What number did I think of?

.... [2]

PS **8** Here is a triangle.

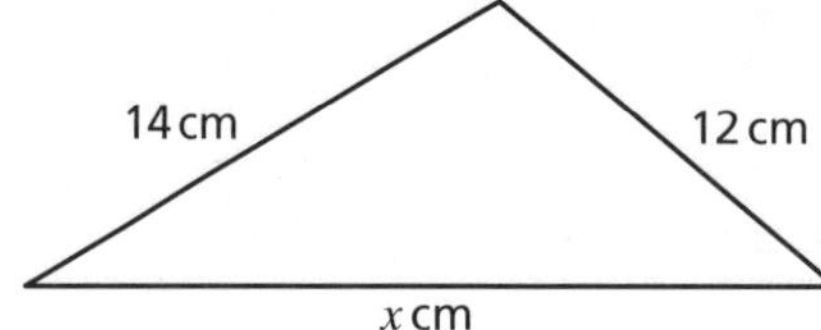

a) Write down an expression, in terms of x, for the perimeter of the triangle.

.... [1]

b) The perimeter of the triangle is 46 cm.

Write down an equation for x. .... [1]

c) Work out the value of x.

$x =$ .... [1]

PS **9** Each of these boxes contains the same total mass.

Box 1	Box 2	Box 3
5 g, 5 g, 5 g, 10 g, 20 g	5 g, 5 g, 10 g, x g, 20 g	10 g, 5 g, y g, y g, y g

Work out the values of x and y.

$x =$ ....

$y =$ .... [4]

Total Marks .... / 38

MR **1** **a)** In this number wall, the value in each brick is the sum of the values in the two bricks below.

Complete the number wall to show that an expression for the value in the top brick is $x + 32$

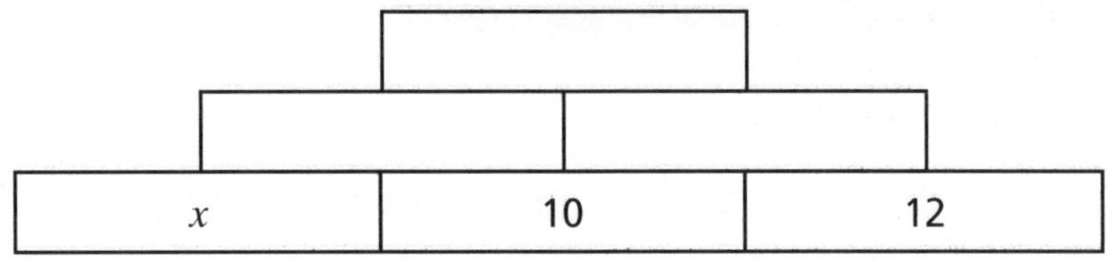

[2]

b) If the number in the top brick is 43, write down an equation for x.

.... [1]

c) Work out the value of x.

$x =$ .... [1]

2 For each diagram, write down an equation to work out the size of the lettered angle.

a)

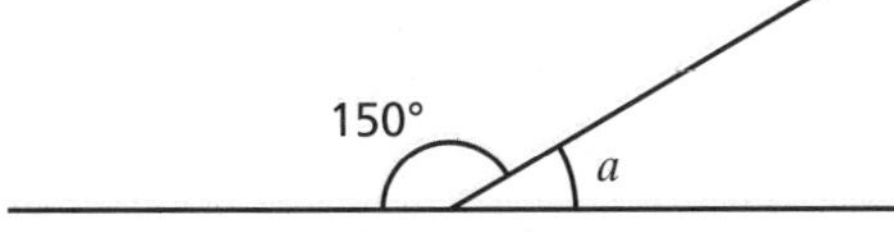

$a =$ .... ° [2]

b)

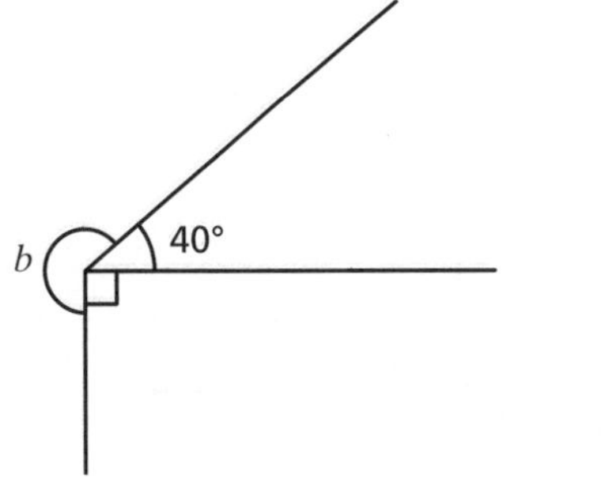

$b =$ .... ° [2]

c)

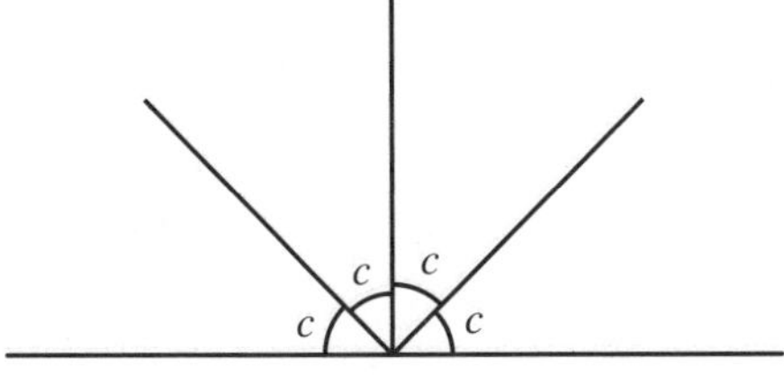

$c =$ .... ° [2]

3 Fill in the missing values in each of the following equations.

a) 3 × 7 + 4 = ☐

b) 3 × 5 – ☐ = 14

c) 3 × ☐ + 2 = 17

d) 3 × ☐ – 1 = 20

e) 3 × ☐ – 5 = 19

f) 6 × ☐ – 5 = 25

[6]

Total Marks .... / 16

Equations

Video Solution Question 2

(MR) **1** Jon is 2 years older than Matt.

a) If Matt is m years old, write down an expression for Jon's age.

.... [1]

b) Jon and Matt's total age is 70 years.

Write an equation, in terms of m, to show this.

.... [1]

c) Show that Jon is 36 years old.

....

.... [2]

(PS) **2** This is a plan of an office space.
The shape has two lines of symmetry.

2 m
2 m
5 m
x m

a) Show that an expression for the perimeter is $(2x + 26)$ m

....

.... [2]

b) Work out the perimeter when $x = 12$

.... m [2]

c) Show that an expression for the area is $(9x + 20)\,\text{m}^2$

....

.... [2]

d) Work out the area when $x = 12$

.... m^2 [2]

Total Marks .... / 12

.... / 38

.... / 16

.... / 12

How do you feel about these skills?

Green = Got it!
Orange = Nearly there
Red = Needs practice

Pie Charts

Video Solution Question 2

MR 1 The pie chart shows the favourite breakfast drinks of 40 adults. The number who said juice is half of the number who said coffee.

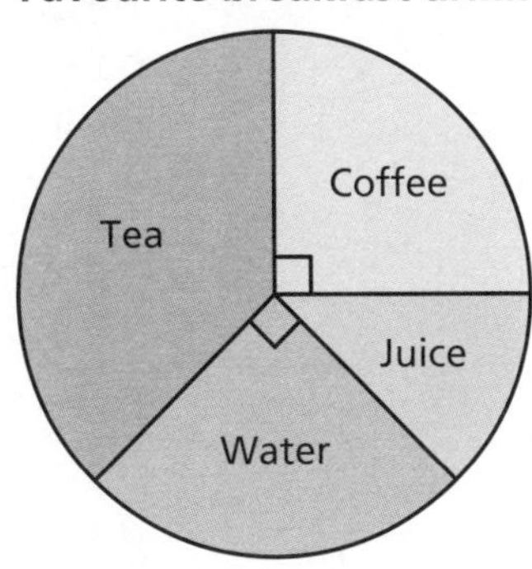

Work out how many chose each drink.

Coffee: ....

Juice: ....

Water: ....

Tea: .... [4]

MR 2 The pie chart shows the favourite colour of 100 students. 40% said blue was their favourite colour. The percentage who said green is half the percentage who said blue.

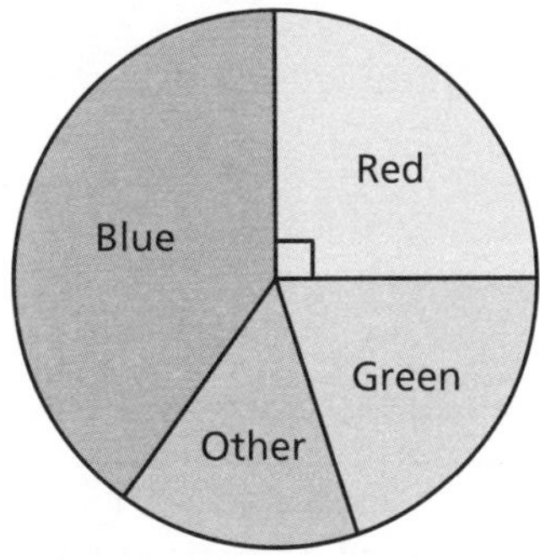

Complete the percentages for each choice.

Blue: 40%

Red: ....%

Green: ....%

Other: ....% [4]

Total Marks .... / 8

Pie Charts

Video Solution Question 2

(PS) **1** The pie chart shows the types of pet owned by a group of students, as percentages.

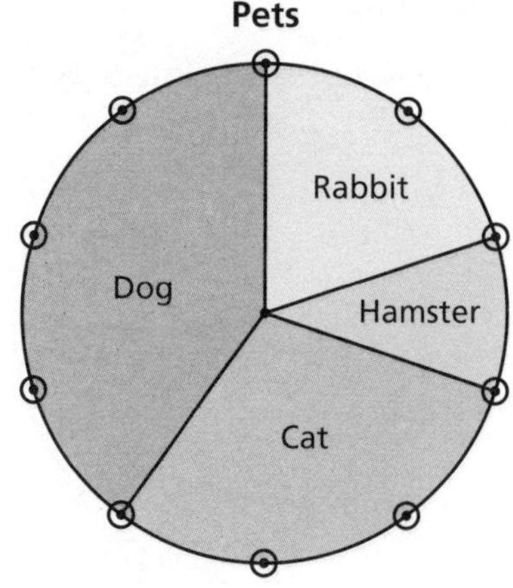

a) What percentage of the pets are dogs? .... % [1]

b) What percentage of the pets are cats? .... % [1]

c) What percentage of the pets are rabbits or hamsters? .... % [1]

d) There are 6 cats.

How many pets are there altogether? .... [1]

e) Andy says, "The total number of cats and rabbits is the same as the number of dogs."

Is he correct? Show how you decide.

....

.... [2]

2 The table shows the distribution of age groups in a small town.

Age	Under 16	16–40	41–60	Over 60
Percentage	10%	30%	40%	20%

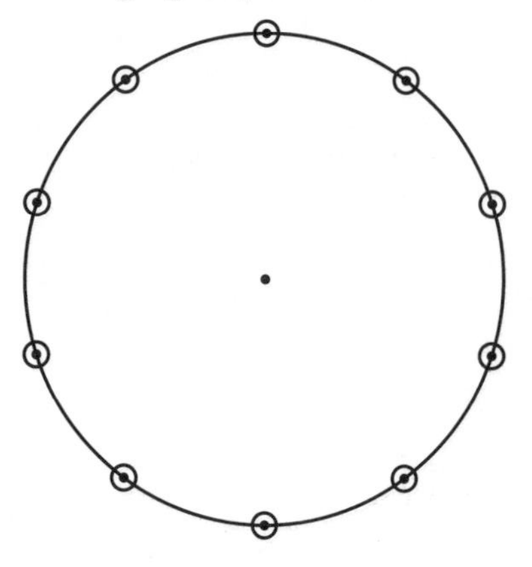

a) Show the information on the pie chart. [3]

b) There are 4700 people in the town.

How many are over 60? .... [2]

c) What percentage of the people are over 40?

.... % [1]

Total Marks .... / 12

PS **1** The pie chart shows the number of children in 80 households on one street.

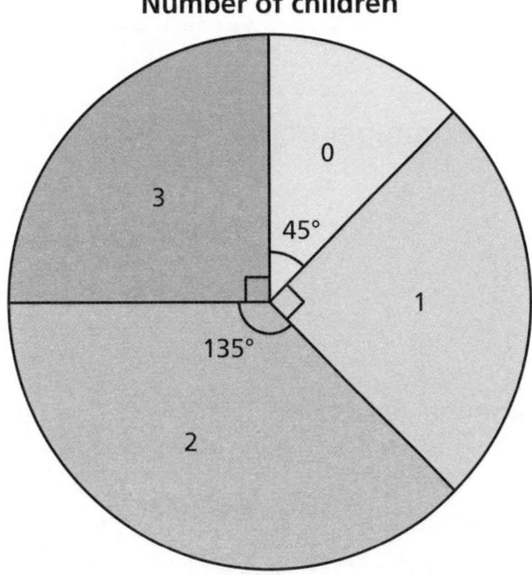

a) Work out the number of households with no children.

.... [2]

b) Work out the number of children in the 80 households altogether.

.... [3]

c) Work out the mean number of children per household.

.... [2]

Total Marks .... / 7

	.... / 8
	.... / 12
	.... / 7

How do you feel about these skills?

Green = Got it!
Orange = Nearly there
Red = Needs practice

3D Shapes

Video Solution Question 3

1 For this cuboid, write down the number of:

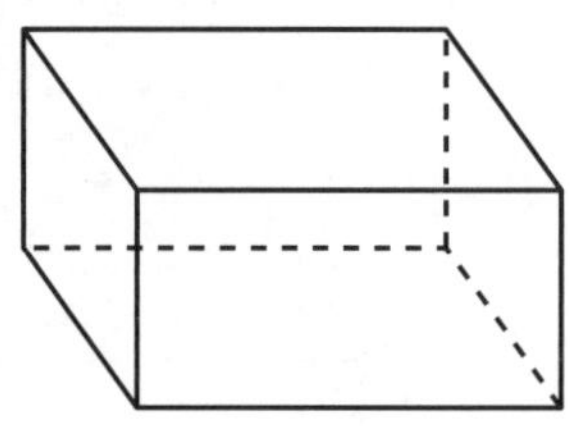

a) faces .... [1]

b) vertices .... [1]

c) edges .... [1]

2 Here are eight 3D shapes labelled A to H.

A

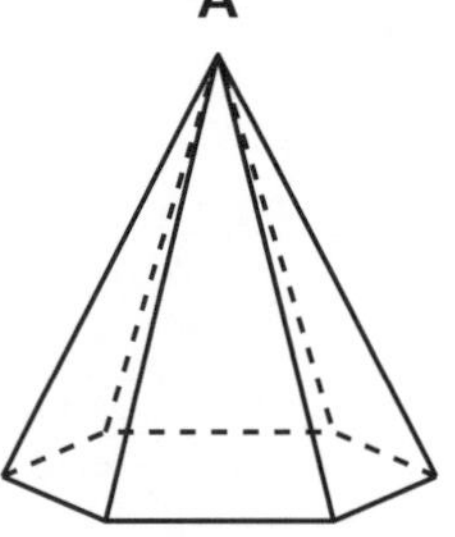

B

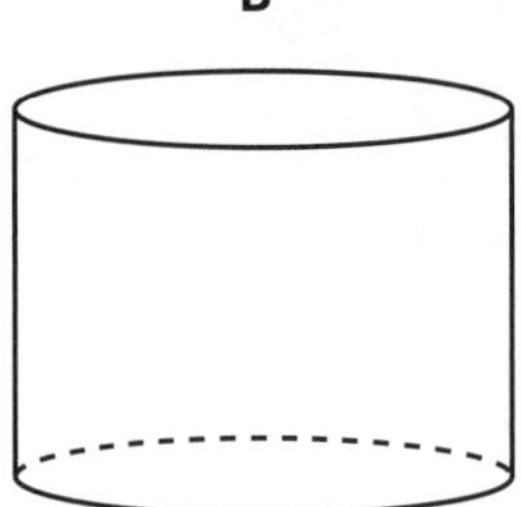

C

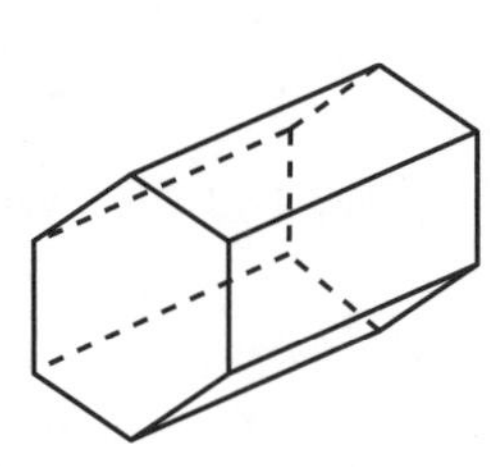

D

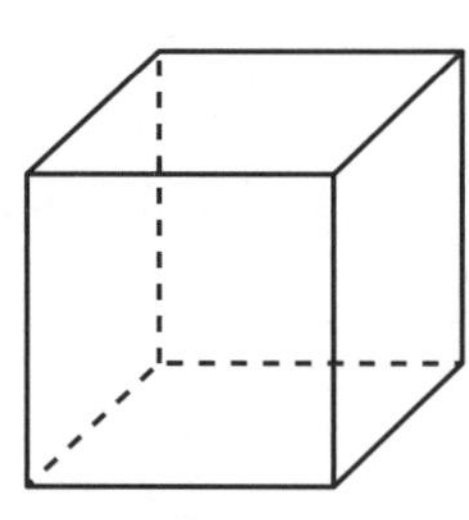

E

F

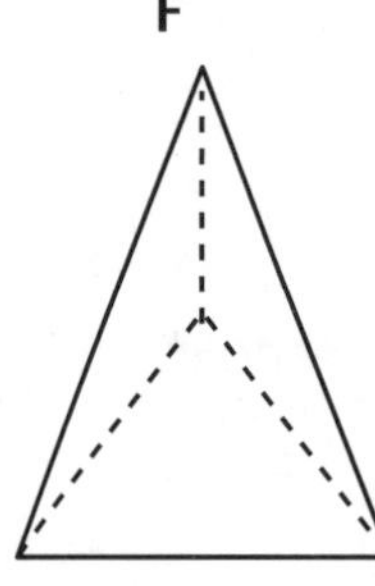

G

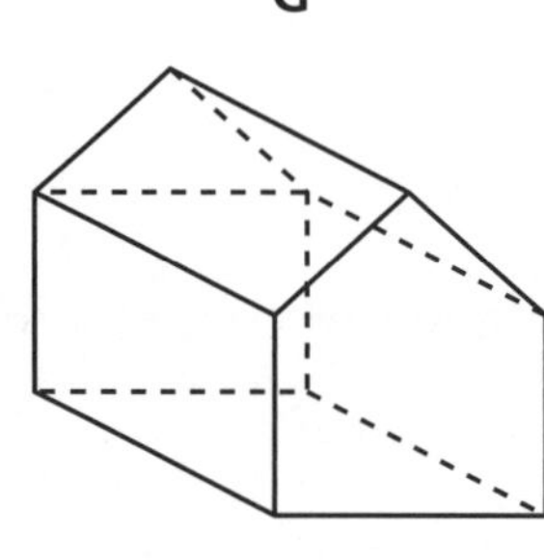

H

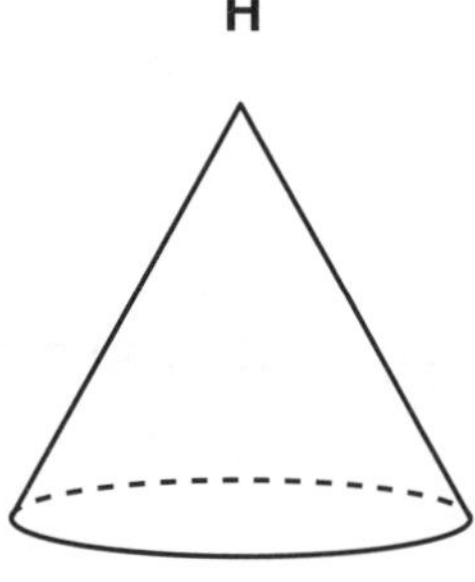

a) Which shape has ten vertices? .... [1]

b) Which shape has nine edges? .... [1]

c) Which shape has the same number of faces as shape G? .... [1]

d) Which shape has twice as many vertices as shape E? .... [1]

e) How many shapes have a face which is not flat? .... [1]

f) Which shape is a pentagonal prism? .... [1]

g) Which shape has the greatest number of vertices? .... [1]

h) What is the name of shape B? .... [1]

3 Work out the volume of this cube.

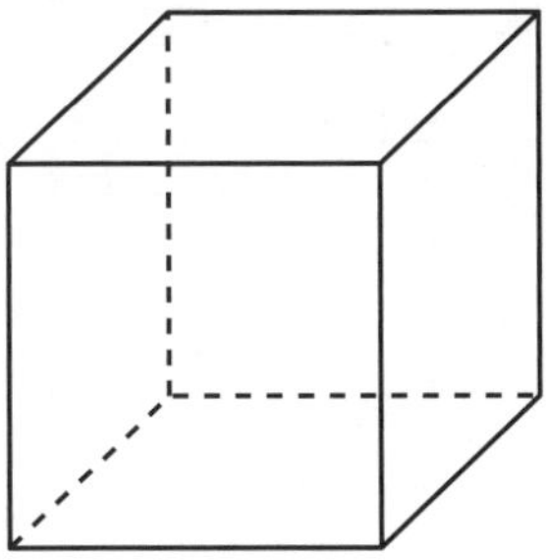

4 cm

.... cm^3 [2]

4 This solid has been made using 1 cm cubes.

What is the volume of the solid?

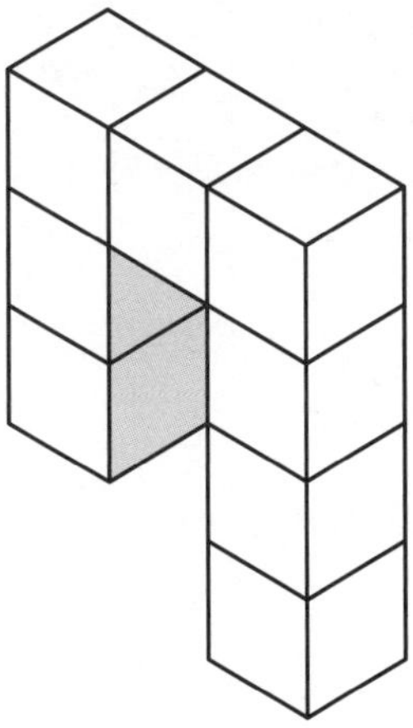

.... cm^3 [1]

Total Marks .... / 14

1 Sketch the net of a triangular prism.

[2]

2 Which shape, P or Q, has more vertices and by how many?

....

.... [2]

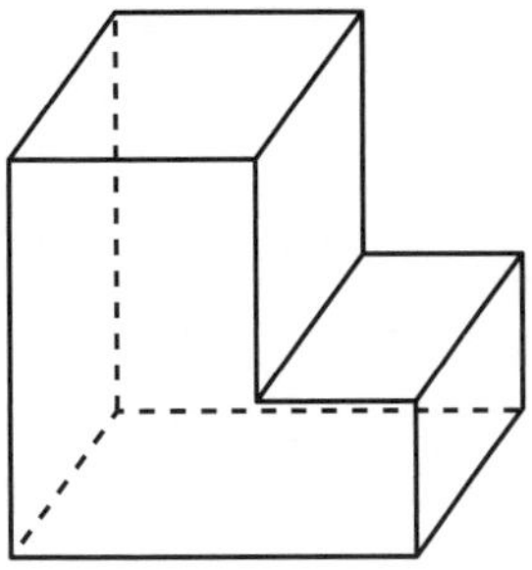

P

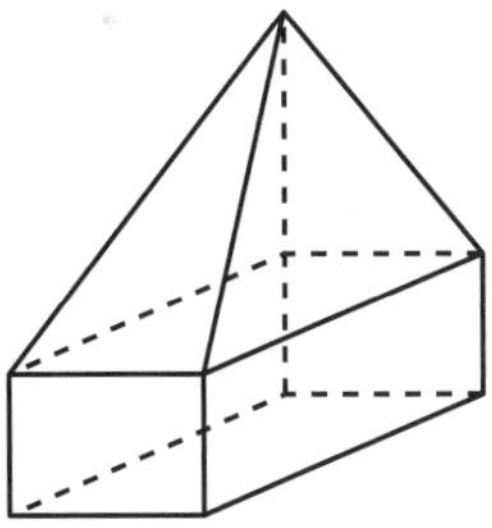

Q

MR **3** Here are four nets labelled A to D.

A

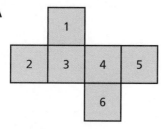

B

C

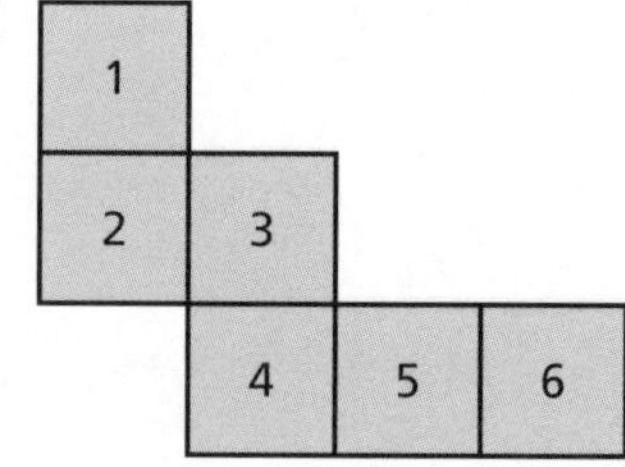

D

a) Which net above will **not** make a cube? .... [2]

b) For each net in part a) that will make a cube, which of the faces 2, 3, 4, 5 or 6 would be opposite face 1 when folded?

.... [3]

MR **4** A section of a pyramid is cut off (shaded on the diagram).

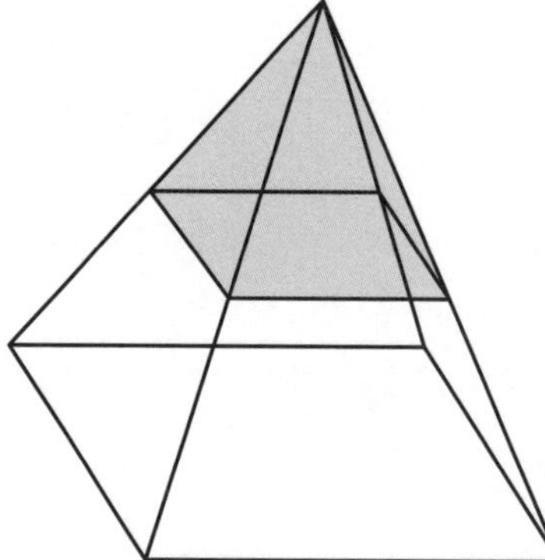

How many vertices, faces and edges does the remaining bottom part have?

.... vertices

.... faces

.... edges [3]

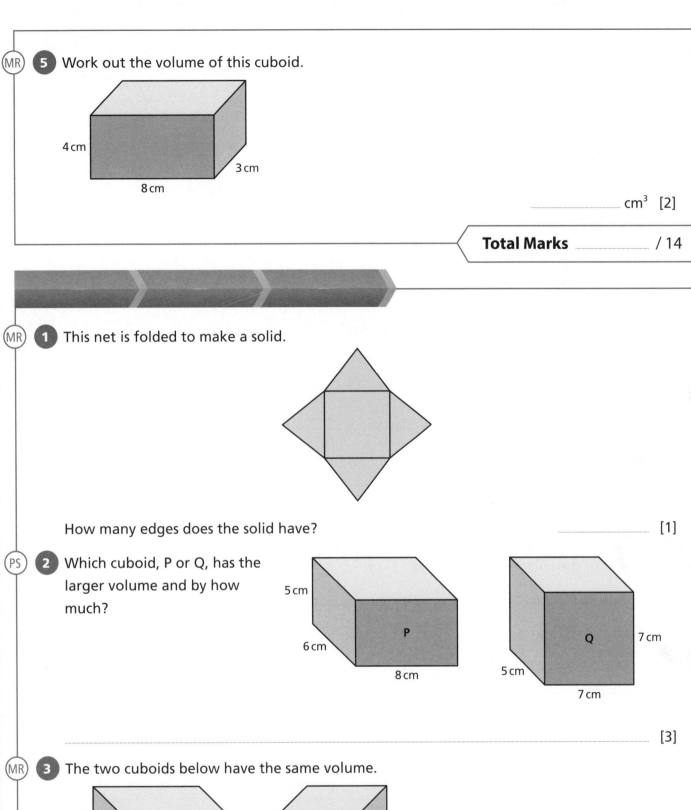

(MR) **5** Work out the volume of this cuboid.

4 cm
3 cm
8 cm

.... cm^3 [2]

Total Marks .... / 14

(MR) **1** This net is folded to make a solid.

How many edges does the solid have? .... [1]

(PS) **2** Which cuboid, P or Q, has the larger volume and by how much?

5 cm
P
6 cm
8 cm

Q
7 cm
5 cm
7 cm

.... [3]

(MR) **3** The two cuboids below have the same volume.

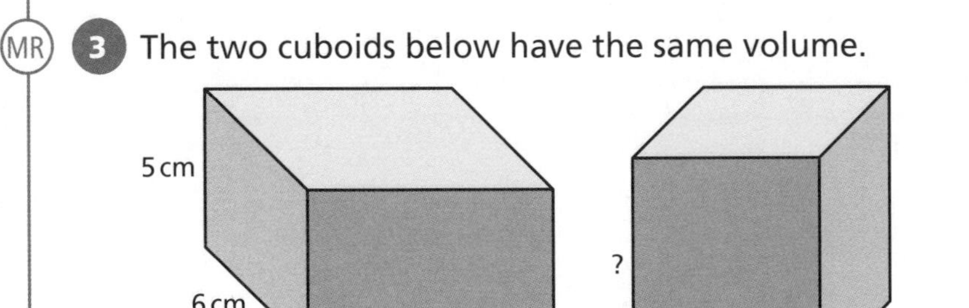

Work out the height of the second cuboid.

.... cm [2]

PS **4** Water is poured into the tank shown at a rate of 50 cm^3 each second.

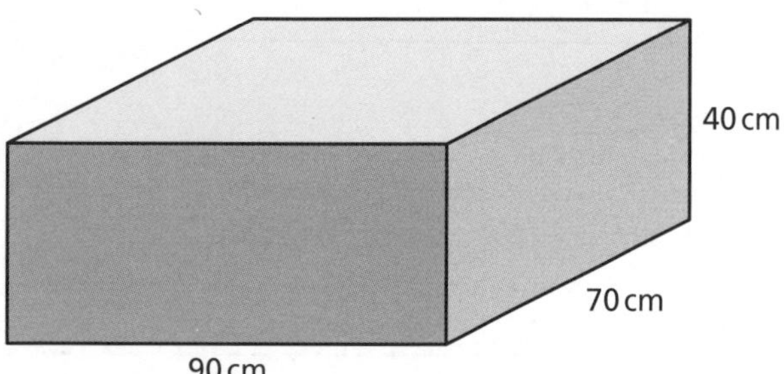

How many minutes will it take to fill the tank?

.... minutes [4]

MR **5** The areas of three faces of a cuboid are shown.

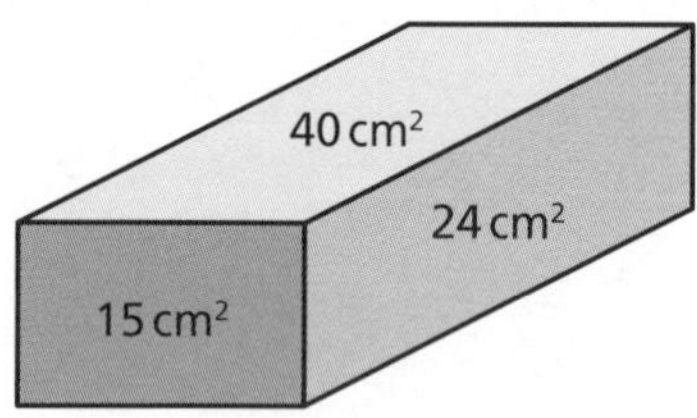

Work out the volume of the cuboid.

.... cm^3 [3]

Total Marks .... / 13

	.... / 14
	.... / 14
	.... / 13

How do you feel about these skills?	
PS MR	Green = Got it! Orange = Nearly there Red = Needs practice

Ratio

Video Solution Question 2

1 Shade squares in each grid to show the given ratio.

a) Black to white 3 : 7

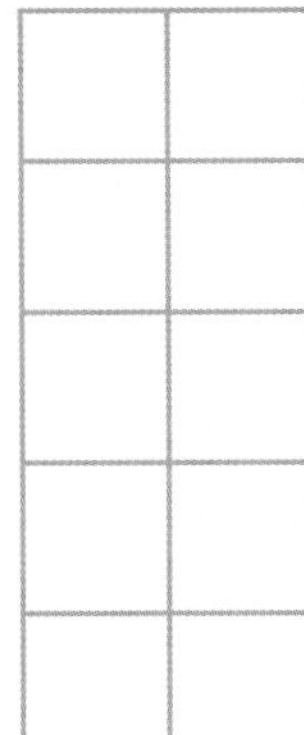

b) Black to white 2 : 3

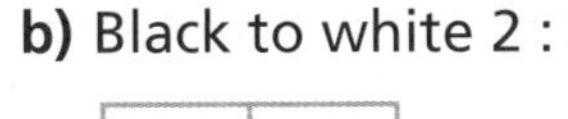

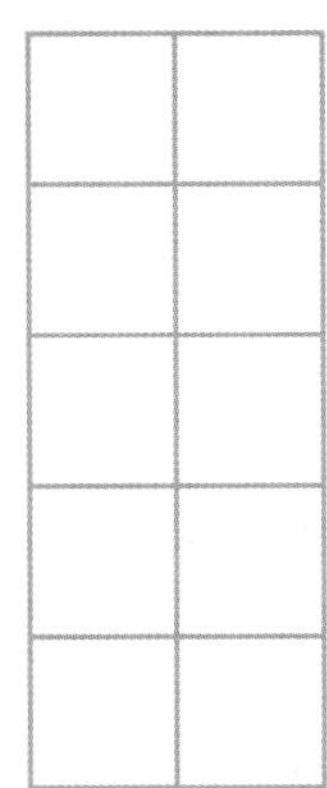

c) Black to white 5 : 3

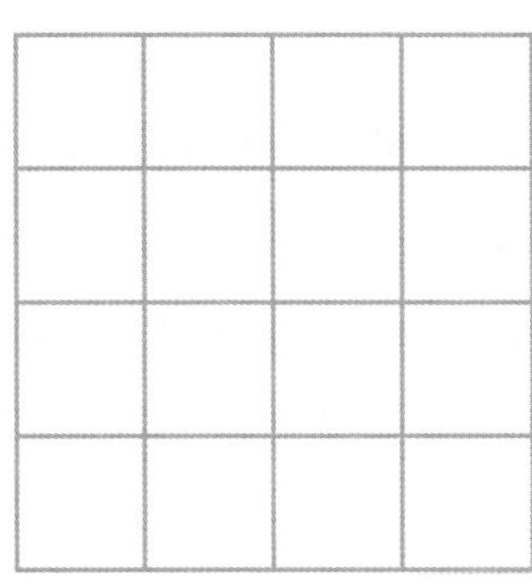

[3]

2 a) Amit and Bill share £21 in the ratio 2 : 5

How much does each person get?

Amit: £ ....

Bill: £ .... [2]

b) Cory and Daisy share 200 g of sweets in the ratio 3 : 5

How much does each person get?

Cory: .... g

Daisy: .... g [2]

3 330 ml of orange paint is made from red and yellow paint in the ratio 4 : 7

a) How much red paint is used?

.... ml [1]

b) How much yellow paint is used?

.... ml [1]

MR 4 Write in the multiplicative relationships shown by the arrows in each ratio table.

a)

× ......

× ......

1	5
3	15

× ......

× ......

b)

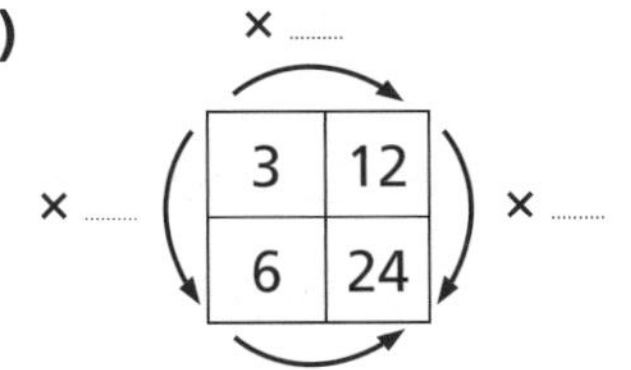

c)

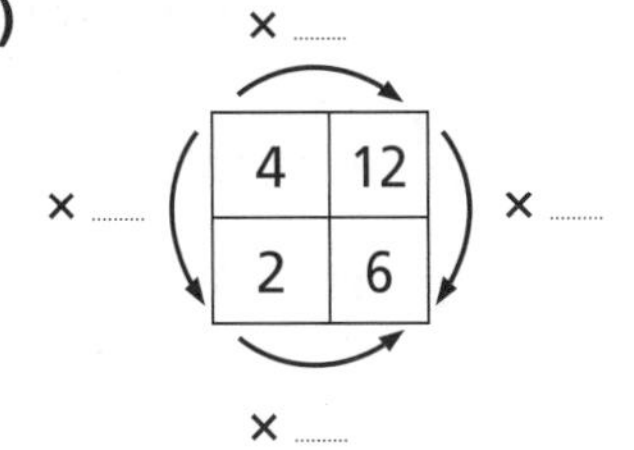

[6]

Video Solution Question 3

5 This double number line can be used to convert between pounds (£) and euros (€).
£5 is equivalent to €6.

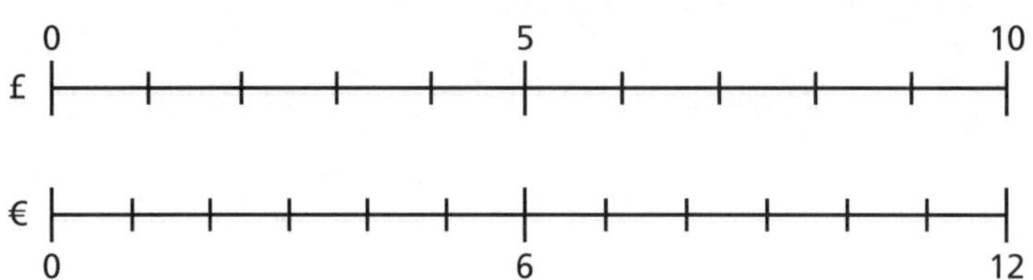

Use the double number line to:

a) convert 12 euros to pounds £ .... [1]

b) estimate the number of euros that are equivalent to £3 € .... [1]

6 5 miles = 8 km

a) Complete this double number line to convert between miles and kilometres.

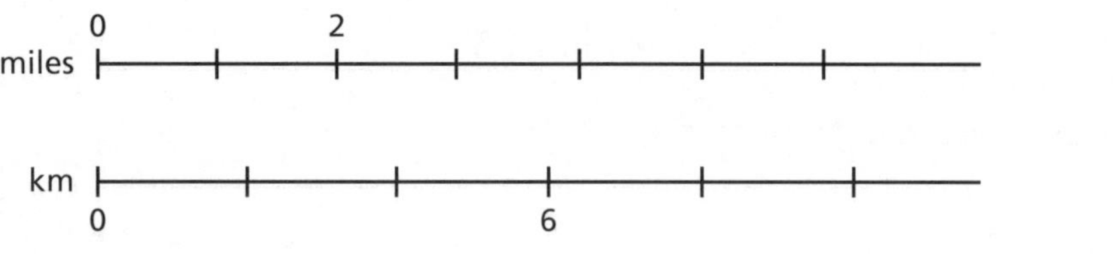

[2]

b) Which is greater, 4 km or 3 miles? .... [1]

7 Eli and Flo share 18 stickers in the ratio 2 : 7

What fraction of the 18 stickers does Flo get? .... [1]

Total Marks .... / 21

MR **1** Gina and Harry share 27 counters in the ratio 4 : 5

Complete each statement with a fraction in its simplest form.

a) Gina's share is $\frac{\square}{\square}$ of Harry's share. [1]

b) Harry's share is $\frac{\square}{\square}$ of Gina's share. [1]

c) Harry's share is $\frac{\square}{\square}$ of the total number of counters. [1]

MR **2** Put a tick (✔) by any table below that shows a proportional relationship.

Put a cross (✘) by any table that does not show a proportional relationship.

a)

3	9
12	36

b)

7	4
21	63

c)

5	2.5
25	0.5

[3]

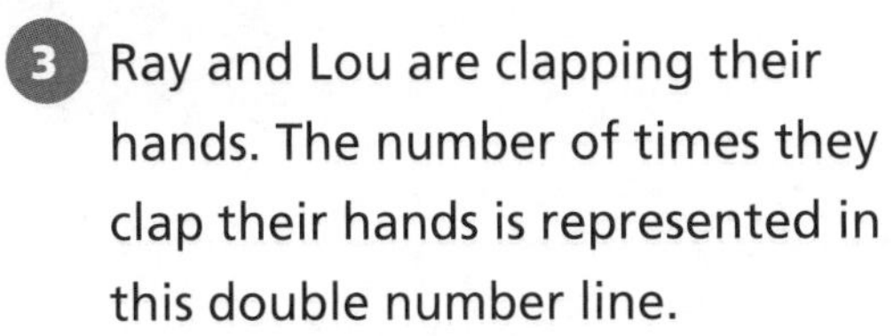

3 Ray and Lou are clapping their hands. The number of times they clap their hands is represented in this double number line.

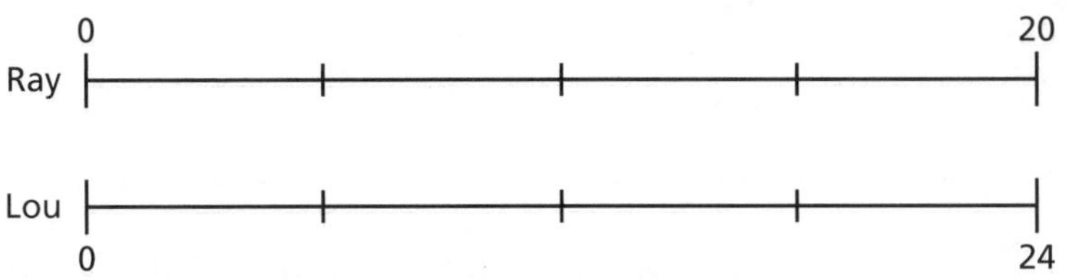

a) Use the double number line to help you complete this table for Ray and Lou's claps:

20	10	
24		6

[2]

b) Ray's 20th clap was at exactly the same time as Lou's 24th clap.

When else did they both clap at exactly the same time?

.... [2]

c) When will they next clap at the same time?

.... [1]

PS **4** Izzy and Jake share some mints in the ratio 4 : 3

Izzy gets 5 more mints than Jake.

How many mints does Jake get?

.... [2]

5 Shade squares in each grid to show the given ratio.

a) Black to grey to white 1 : 3 : 6

b) Black to grey to white 3 : 5 : 2

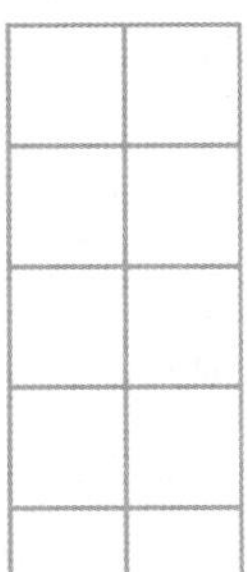

c) Black to white to grey 1: 2: 5

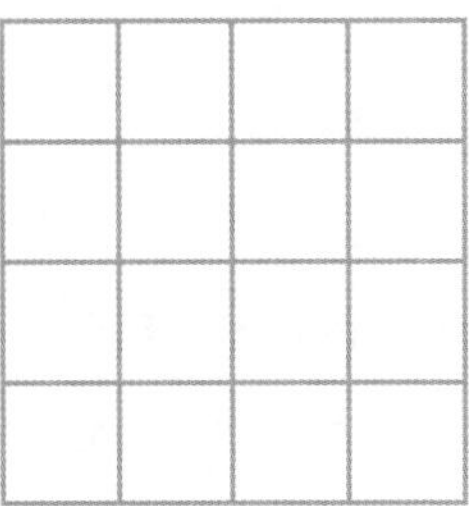

[6]

Total Marks .... / 19

MR **1** This double number line converts between pounds and kilograms.

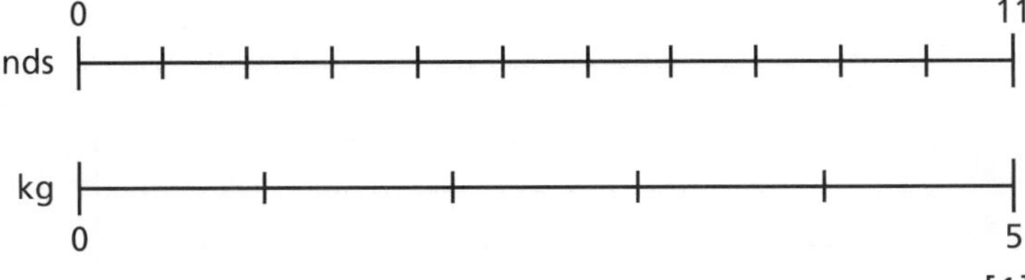

Complete these statements.

a) 5 kg = ... pounds [1]

b) 1 pound = ... kg [1]

Ratio

MR **2** In each ratio table, write in the multiplicative relationships shown by the arrows, and any missing numbers.

a) × ....

× ....

3	1
12	

× ....

× ....

b) × ....

× ....

5	2
15	6

× ....

× ....

c) × ....

× ....

4	5
	1.25

× ....

× ....

[6]

PS **3** Max and Nora share some toffees in the ratio 3 : 7
Max gets 8 fewer toffees than Nora.

How many toffees does Nora get?

.... [3]

MR FS **4** The graph shows the exchange rate between pounds (£) and Australian dollars (Aus $).

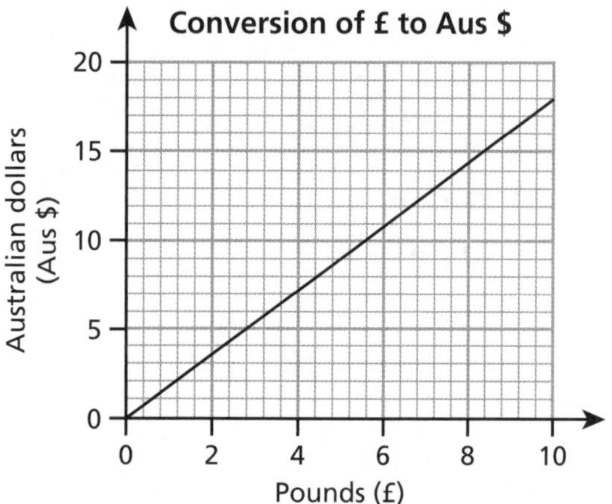

Complete this statement:

The graph shows that the exchange rate is Aus $........ for every £5 [1]

PS **5** Oli makes a drink from squash and water in the ratio 1 : 7
Polly makes a drink from the same squash and water in the ratio 3 : 17

Whose drink has a higher proportion of squash? Show your working.

.... [3]

Total Marks .... / 15

	.... / 21
	.... / 19
	.... / 15

How do you feel about these skills?

PS MR FS

Green = Got it!
Orange = Nearly there
Red = Needs practice

Answers

Pages 4–7: Number Properties

1. a) four hundred and ninety-seven thousand and sixteen [1]
   b) 3 024 102 [1]
2. a) 824 520 [1] b) 825 000 [1] c) 820 000 [1]
3. a) 8 [1] b) 11 [1] c) 2 [1] d) 9 [1]
4. a) 49 [1] b) 64 [1] c) 144 [1] d) 27 [1]
5. a) 2^5 [1] b) 3^4 [1]
6. First work out the powers, then multiply.

   a) $2^3 \times 5^2 = 8 \times 25$ [1] $= 200$ [1]
   b) $3^2 \times 2^3 = 9 \times 8$ [1] $= 72$ [1]
   c) $9^2 \times 10^2 = 81 \times 100$ [1] $= 8100$ [1]
   d) $2 \times 3^3 \times 5 = 2 \times 27 \times 5 = 27 \times 10$ [1] $= 270$ [1]
7. a) 1, 2, 3, 6, 9, 27 [2]
   [1 mark for at least three correct or if extra incorrect values are included]
   b) 4, 8, 20, 28 [2]
   [1 mark for at least three correct or if extra incorrect values are included]
   c) 2, 7 [2]
   [1 mark for 2 or 7, or if extra incorrect values are included]
8. a) 60 [1] b) 15 [1] c) 36 or 60 [1]
9. a)

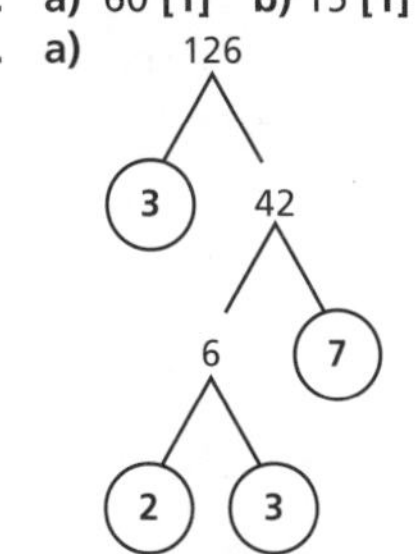

[4]
   [1 mark for each]
   b) $2 \times 3^2 \times 7$ or $2 \times 3 \times 3 \times 7$ [1]

1. a) 1000 [1] b) 408 700 [1]
2. $\sqrt[3]{27}$ $\sqrt{24}$ $\sqrt[3]{125}$ $\sqrt{49}$ [1]
3. 1000 [1]
4. a) 2^3 [1] b) 2^5 [1] c) 2^7 [1] d) 2^8 [1]
5. The smallest number with prime factors 2, 3, 5 and 7 $= 2 \times 3 \times 5 \times 7$

   210 [1]
6. First work out the powers, then subtract.

   $5^3 - 6^2 = 125 - 36$ [1] $= 89$ [1]
7. 7.02 m, 2.7 m, 2070 mm, 20.07 cm, 2.07 cm [2]
   [1 mark if only one value is incorrectly placed]
8. Round each number to the nearest thousand, then add.

   3000 + 159 000 [1] = 162 000 [1]
9. a) HCF is the product of the numbers in the intersection.

   $2 \times 3^2 = 18$ [1]

   b)

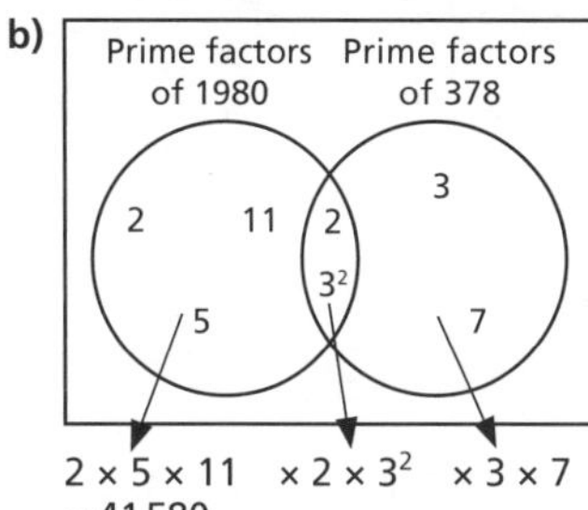

LCM is the product of the numbers in both circles, only including the ones in the intersection once.

$2 \times 5 \times 11 \times 2 \times 3^2 \times 3 \times 7$ [1]
$= 41 580$ [1]

1. 15 m = 3 mm × 5 × 1000
   3 mm is 5000 times shorter than 15 m
   5000 [1]
2. $7^2 - 4^2$ [1]
   $= 49 - 16 = 33 \text{ cm}^2$ [1]
3.

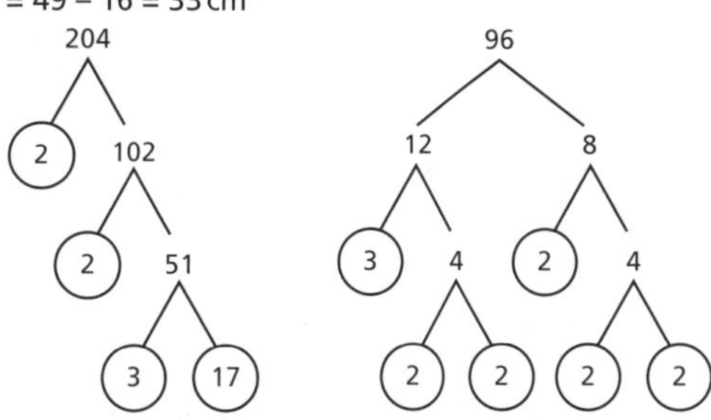

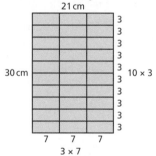

$204 = 2^2 \times 3 \times 17$ [1] $96 = 2^5 \times 3$ [1]
HCF $= 2^2 \times 3 = 12$ [1]
4. $3 \times 5 \times 7 = 105$ [1]
5. Common multiples of 3, 4 and 12 are the multiples of 12:
   12, 24, 36, 48, 60, 72, 84, 96, 108, … [1]
   The greatest two-digit multiple of 12 is 96
   96 [1]
6. Drives 84 km every weekday, so approx 80 km
   In 6 weeks, there are 30 weekdays
   30 × 80 [1] = 2400 km [1]
7. Lowest common multiple of 12 and 15 is 60 [1]
   10:01 [1]
8. a) Attempt to work out the HCF of 84, 132 and 180 [1]
   12 boxes needed [1]
   b) Blue: 7, Red: 11, Yellow: 15 [2]
   [1 mark for any two values correct]
9. 21 cm
   30 cm
   3 3 3 3 3 3 3 3 3 3
   10 × 3
   7 7 7
   3 × 7

   30 [2] **[1 mark for 3 × 10]**

Pages 8–11: Sequences

1. a) 16, 19 [1] b) −5, −1, 2, 6 [1]
   c) 10, 14 and 9, 11 [1] d) 11, 7 and 12, 6 [1]
2. a) − 5 [1] b) ÷ 5 [1]
3. a) $7 \times 4 - 3 = 28 - 3 = 25$ [1] b) $-2 \times 4 - 3 = -8 - 3 = -11$ [1]
   c) $(5 + 3) \div 4 = 8 \div 4 = 2$ [1] d) $(9 + 3) \div 4 = 12 \div 4 = 3$ [1]
4. a) 8, 20, 32, 44, 56 [1] b) 24, 15, 6, −3, −12 [1]
   c) 1, 2, 4, 8, 16 [1] d) 32, 16, 8, 4, 2 [1]
5. a)

[1]
   Number of sticks in pattern 5 is 5 × 4 = 20 [1]
   b) [1]
   Number of sticks in pattern 5 is 5 × 5 = 25 [1]

1. a) 6, 0 [1]; subtract 6 [1]
   b) 9, 4.5 [1]; divide by 2 [1]
   c) 81, 243 [1]; multiply by 3 [1]
   d) 7.5, 9 [1]; add 1.5 [1]

2. a) A [1] b) B [1] c) $\frac{1}{1000}$ or 0.001 [1] d) B [1]
3. 22, 25, 28, 31, 34, so the 10th term is 34. [1]
The 5th term is 19, so double 5th term = 38 (not 34) [1]

1. 15, 40 [1] 115, 140 [1]
2. a) 3, 10, 17, 24 [1]
b) Six terms [1]
3 + 10 + 17 + 24 + 31 + 38 = 123 [1]
3. a) 1 + 3 + 5 + 7 + 9 = 25 = 5^2 [1]
b) 10^2 = 100 [1]
4. 71, 63, 55, 47, 39, 31, 23, 15, ... (subtract 8) [1]
2.5, 5, 7.5, 10, 12.5, 15, ... (add 2.5) [1]
15 [1]

Pages 12–16: Perimeter and Area

1. 36 – 17 – 7 = 12 mm [1]
2. 18 + 24 [1] = 42 cm [1]
3. Perimeter = 24 cm [1] Area = 15 cm^2 [1]
4. 9 cm [1]
5. a) Q (36 cm^2) [1] has a greater area than P (35 cm^2) [1] by 1 cm^2 [1]
b) Q (26 cm) [1] has a greater perimeter than P (24 cm) [1] by 2 cm [1]
6. a) Length of one side = 7 mm [1] b) Area = 7 × 7 = 49 mm^2 [1]
7. $\frac{1}{2}$(18 × 7) = 63 cm^2 [1]

1. Width = 6 mm [1]
Area = 8 × 6 = 48 mm^2 [1]
2. Area A = 12 × 9 = 108 cm^2 [1]
Area B = 15 × 12 = 180 cm^2 [1]
Total area = 288 cm^2 [1]
3. a) $\frac{1}{2}$ × 6 × (7 + 15) [1] = 66 cm^2 [1]
b) 12 × 8 [1] = 96 cm^2 [1]
4. If 6 cm is the base then the height is 8 cm not 10 cm [1]
Area should be $\frac{1}{2}$ × (6 × 8) = 24 cm^2 [1]
[Full marks if it is made clear that 10 cm should not be used.]
5. Area rectangle = 10 × 12 = 120 cm^2 [1]
Area triangle = $\frac{1}{2}$ × (4 × 6) = 12 cm^2 [1]
Shaded area = 120 – 12 = 108 cm^2 [1]
6. a) One side = 6 m [1] Perimeter = 24 m [1]
b) Cost = 24 × 9 = £216 [1]

1. $\frac{1}{2}$ × base × 16 = 72 or base = 72 ÷ 8 [1]
= 9 cm [1]

$\frac{1}{2}$(base × height) = 72 so base × height = 144

2. a) square (36 cm^2) [1] + triangle (18 cm^2) = 54 cm^2 [1]
b) $\frac{1}{2}$(13 + 5) × 8 or 9 × 8 or 18 × 4 [1]
= 72 cm^2 [1]

Use area = $\frac{1}{2}h(a + b)$ or split shape into triangles and/or rectangles.

3. a) Missing sides are 7 + 4 = 11 cm and 9 + 5 = 14 cm [1]
Perimeter: 5 + 11 + 14 + 7 + 9 + 4 = 50 cm [1]
Area: (7 × 9) + (5 × 11) or (5 × 4) + (14 × 7) [1]
= 118 cm^2 [1]
b) Missing sides are 7 cm, 3 cm, 3 cm, 3 cm and 3 cm [1]
Perimeter: 2 + 7 + 3 + 3 + 8 + 3 + 3 + 7 = 36 cm [1]
Area: (8 × 3) + (7 × 2) [1]
= 38 cm^2 [1]
c) Missing sides are 18 – 6 – 3 = 9 cm and 8 + 8 – 11 = 5 cm [1]
Perimeter: 3 + 8 + 9 + 5 + 6 + 8 + 18 + 11 = 68 cm [1]
Area: (11 × 3) + (3 × 9) + (6 × 8) [1]
= 108 cm^2 [1]
4. Area = $\frac{1}{2}$ × 3 × (5 + 7) = 18 m^2 [1]
18 ÷ 4 = 4.5 so 5 tins needed [1]
Cost = £100 [1]

Whole tins of paint must be bought.

5. Area rectangle = 9 × 13 = 117 cm^2 [1]
Area triangle = $\frac{1}{2}$ × (5 × 9) = 22.5 cm^2 and
Area trapezium = $\frac{1}{2}$ × 9 × (6 + 11) = 76.5 cm^2 or Area parallelogram = 9 × 2 = 18 cm^2 [1]
117 – 18 or 22.5 + 76.5 [1]
Unshaded area = 99 cm^2 [1]
6. Area = $\frac{1}{2}$ × 4 × (10 + ?) = 28 [1] so bottom length = 4 cm [1]
Perimeter = $2n$ + 10 + 4 = 24 [1] so n = 5 cm [1]

Pages 17–20: Decimal Numbers

1. a) 9 tenths or $\frac{9}{10}$ [1] b) 6 hundredths or $\frac{6}{100}$ [1]
2. a) 268 [1]

An integer is a whole number.

b) 267.8 [1] c) 267.84 [1]
3. a) 0.076 [1] b) 0.006 [1] c) 0.176 [1] d) 0.026 [1]
4. a) 37 [1] b) 1540 [1] c) 0.2 [1] d) 0.342 [1] e) 500.7 [1] f) 0.059 [1] g) 60.25 [1] h) 0.05 [1] i) 0.9 [1]
5. 3.09, 3.146, 3.15, 3.2, 3.271, 3.4 [2]
[1 mark if only one value is incorrectly placed]
6. a) $\frac{1}{10}$ [1] b) $\frac{1}{100}$ [1] c) $\frac{1}{1000}$ [1]
7. a) 15.65 [1] b) 15.6 [1]
8. a) 435 cm [1] b) 1600 ml [1] c) 0.25 kg [1] d) 1.5 km [1] e) 3.65 litres [1] f) 4800 g [1] g) 0.176 tonnes [1] h) 0.85 m [1] i) 14.26 km [1]

1 m = 1000 mm	1 km = 1000 m	1 tonne = 1000 kg
1 m = 100 cm	1 kg = 1000 g	1 litre = 1000 ml

1. a) 0.245 [1] b) 6 [1]
2. a)
$$\begin{array}{r} 47.326 \\ +\ 9.095 \\ \hline 56.421 \end{array}$$
b)
$$\begin{array}{r} 513.125 \\ -\ 241.386 \\ \hline 271.739 \end{array}$$
[7] **[1 mark for each value]**
3. 100 000 [1]
4. a) Multiplying by 0.1 is equivalent to dividing by **10** [1]
b) Multiplying by 0.001 is equivalent to dividing by **1000** [1]
c) Dividing by 0.1 is equivalent to multiplying by **10** [1]
d) Dividing by 0.01 is equivalent to multiplying by **100** [1]
5. a) 1.2 [1] b) 0.032 [1] c) 0.065 [1] d) 560 [1] e) 0.27 [1] f) 7 [1] g) 0.529 [1] h) 8000 [1] i) 0.04 [1]
6. 6 × £20 [1] = £120 [1]
7. a) 2.1 [1] b) 0.7 [1] c) 0.032 [1] d) 0.08 [1] e) 0.008 [1] f) 1.2 [1] g) 0.45 [1] h) 0.08 [1] i) 0.3[1]
8. a) 482.6 [1] b) 48.26 [1] c) 48.26 [1] d) 48.26 [1] e) 4.826 [1] f) 4.826 [1]

1. 200 000 [1]
2. a) 0.7 cm [1] b) 35 km [1]
3. 1 tonne = 1000 kg = 50 × 20 kg
50 × £7.85 [1]
= £392.50 [1]
4. a) 1.3 [1] b) 7 [1] c) 0.32 [1] d) 8 [1] e) 1.36 [1] f) 0.0035 [1] g) 0.027 [1] h) 80 [1] i) 0.001 [1]
5. 30 × 0.5 [1]
= £15 [1]
6. a) 3672 [1] b) 136 [1] c) 1360 [1] d) 27 [1] e) 270 [1] f) 0.27 [1]
7. Estimated area of floor: 5 × 3 = 15 m^2 [1]
Estimated number of cans: 15 ÷ 4 = 3.75 [1]
Round up to 4 cans, because 3 cans will not be enough [1]

Pages 21–24: Working with Numbers

1. a) –6 [1] b) –1 [1] c) –4 [1] d) –7 [1] e) –8 [1] f) 3 [1]
2. a) 12 528 [1] b) 273 258 [1]
3. a) 61.75 [1] b) 34.48 [1]
4. Use the order of operations:
Brackets → Powers and roots → Multiplication Division → Addition Subtraction

a) 26 [1] b) 22 [1] c) 7 [1] d) 31 [1] e) 98 [1] f) 39 [1]

5. 17°C [1]
6. £6.70 [1]
7. 5, –1, –7 [3]

1. a) 7 [1] b) –7 [1] c) –1 [1] d) 4 [1] e) –2 [1] f) 19 [1]
2. a) 13.92 [1] b) 125.4 [1]
3. a) 157 [1] b) 34.625 [1]
4. a) 2376 [1] b) 3737 [1] c) 44955 [1]
5. 3.6 × 1.49 = 5.364 [1]
   £5.36 [1]
6. a) 4 [1] b) –64 [1] c) –2 [1]

$(-2)^2 = -2 \times -2$ $(-4)^3 = -4 \times -4 \times -4$

7. a) –14 [1] b) 36 [1] c) –5 [1] d) –3 [1] e) 4 [1] f) 16 [1]
8. 10 hours 40 minutes [1]

1. a) 476.3 [1] b) 485.1 [1] c) 21 [1]
2. 20 jars cost £13 [1]
   10 kg strawberries cost £23, 10 kg sugar costs £8 [1]
   4 lemons cost £1.48 [1]
   Total cost £45.48 [1]
3. 15000 ÷ 330 = 45.45454545… [1]
   (or 15 ÷ 0.33 = 45.45454545…)
   You can fill 45 cups [1]
4. a) 6 [1] b) 1 [1] c) 9 [1] d) 14 [1]
5. 4.6 × 7 [1] = 32.2 cm [1]
6. $(3.2)^3 = 32.768$ [1]
   $32.8\,\text{cm}^3$ [1]

Pages 25–29: Statistics

1. a) 14°C [1]
   b) Winter [1]
2.

Type of travel	Tally	Number of students
Walk	𝍸 𝍸 𝍸	15
Cycle	𝍸 I	6
Bus	𝍸 𝍸 𝍸 𝍸 III	23
Car	𝍸 III	8

[3]

[2 marks for correctly completed final column; 1 mark for correctly completed tally]

3. Total number of people = 5 + 9 + 4 + 10 = 28, so 28 ÷ 4 means 7 per team [1]
   So 3 people move out of team D [1]

1. a)

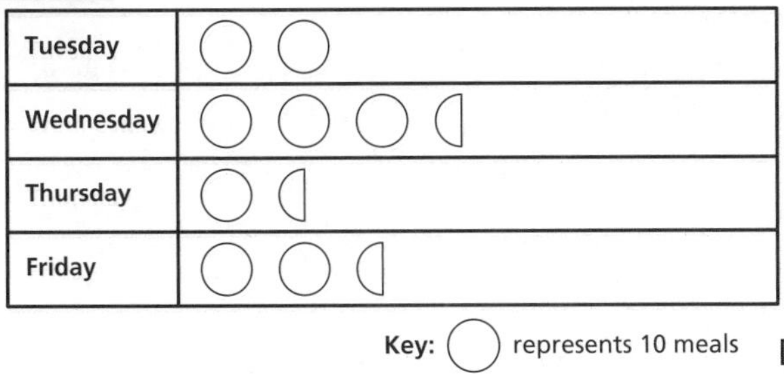

Tuesday	◯ ◯
Wednesday	◯ ◯ ◯ ◖
Thursday	◯ ◖
Friday	◯ ◯ ◖

Key: ◯ represents 10 meals [2]

[1 mark for two rows correct]

   b) Monday sold 35 meals [1]
      35 + 20 + 35 + 15 + 25 = 130 [1]
   c) 130 × £9.50 [1]
      = £1235 [1]
2. 3 × 35 + 2 × 10 or 105 + 20 = £125 [1]
   2 × 35 + 3 × 10 or 70 + 30 = £100 [1] 125 – 100 = £25 [1]
   Alternative method:
   1 fewer adult saves £35 [1]
   1 extra child costs £10 [1]
   Saving is £35 – £10 = £25 [1]

3. a) 50 + 100 + 25 + 75 = 250 True [1] b) 50 + 25 = 75 True [1]
   c) False [1] d) True [1]
4. a)

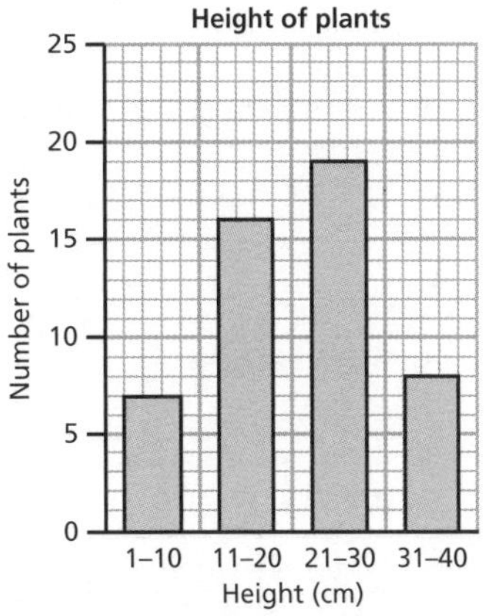

Height of plants

Height (cm)	Number of plants
1–10	7
11–20	16
21–30	19
31–40	8

[2]

[1 mark for at least one correct bar drawn]

   b) 21–30 [1]
   c) All the plants in 31–40 group could be taller than 35 cm [1]
5. a) Mean = (1 + 2 + 4 + 6 + 8 + 9) ÷ 6 [1] = 5 [1]
   b) (11 + 12 + 14 + 16 + 18 + 19) ÷ 6 [1] = 15 [1]
   c) Example answer: Mean is 10 more in part b)
      (as all numbers have increased by 10) [1]
6. a) (8 + 9 + 5 + 6 + 2 + 4 + 3 + 7 + 6 + 6) ÷ 10 or 56 ÷ 10 [1] = 5.6 [1]
   b) (3 + 10 +10 + 2 + 5 + 2 + 3 + 4 + 10 + 2) ÷ 10 or 51 ÷ 10 [1]
      = 5.1 [1]
   c) Asif [1]

1. a)

	Silver	Black	White	Other	Total
Ford	8	11	**10**	9	38
VW	12	**6**	8	**4**	**30**
Toyota	**7**	5	**3**	10	25
Other	13	16	11	7	**47**
Total	40	**38**	**32**	30	140

[4]

[3 marks for 7 or 8 correct values; 2 marks for 5, 6 or 7 correct values; 1 mark for 2, 3 or 4 correct values]

   b) 38 – 32 = 6 [1]
   c) 70 × £1.80 + 70 × £4 or £126 + £280 [1]
      = £406 [1]
2. a) 15 + 10 + 14 [1] = 39 mm [1]
   b) 40 – 39 = 1 mm [1] so only 1 mm of rainfall or not much rainfall [1]
   c) 15 – 10 = 5 mm [1]
3. a) $x + 8 = 10$ [1]
      $x = 2$ [1]
   b) 3, 6, 10, 3, 8 [1]
      Mean = (3 + 3 + 6 + 8 + 10) ÷ 5 or 30 ÷ 5 [1]
      = 6 [1]

Pages 30–34: Algebra

1. a) $3a$ [1] b) $3a + 2b$ [1] c) 0 [1] d) $8x$ [1] e) $8xy$ [1]
   f) $6y$ [1] g) $2x^2 - y$ [2] **[1 mark for each term]**
2. Boxes matched as follows:
   $3x + y + 2x - x$ to $4x + y$
   $3x - 2x$ to x
   $4y - 2x + y - x$ to $-3x + 5y$
   $5x + x - y$ to $6x - y$ [3]
   [2 marks for two correct lines; 1 mark for one correct line]
3. a) $5x + \mathbf{2}y - \mathbf{3}x + 9y = 2x + 11y$ [2]
   b) $9a + 4b - 3c - \mathbf{3}a - \mathbf{6}b + 4c = 6a - 2b + \mathbf{c}$ [3]
4. a) 6 × 4 = 24 [1]
   b) 2 – 7 = –5 [1]
   c) 4 + 2 + 1 = 7 [1]
   d) 3(4 + 5) = 3 × 9 = 27 [1]
   e) 2 × 4 + 3 × 2 – 4 × 1 or 8 + 6 – 4 [1]
      = 10 [1]

5. a) $2y$ **[1]** b) y^2 **[1]** c) $2y^2$ **[1]** d) $6y^2$ **[1]**
e) $2yz$ **[1]** f) xyz **[1]** g) $60xyz$ **[1]** h) t^5 **[1]**

6. a) $3a$ **[1]**
b) $2a + 10$ **[1]**
c) $2a + 2b + c$ **[1]**
d) $2a + 14$ **[1]**
e) $2a + 2b$ or $2(a + b)$ **[1]**
f) $14a$ **[1]**

7. a) $P = 2(4 + 5)$ or $P = 2 \times 9$ **[1]**
$P = 18$ **[1]**
b) $P = 2(6 + 8)$ or $P = 2 \times 14$ **[1]**
$P = 28$ **[1]**
c) Any values for l and w such that $l + w = 12$ **[2]**
[1 mark for each pair]

8. a) $13 \times 3 = £39$ **[1]**
b) $13 \times 4.5 = £58.50$ **[1]**

1. $m = 60h$ **[1]** and $h = \frac{m}{60}$ **[1]**

There are 60 minutes in one hour.

2. $g = 1000k$ There are 1000 grams in a kilogram so, for example, when $k = 2, g = 2000$ (2 kg = 2000 grams) **[1]**

3. a) $T = 2c - w$ **[1]**
b) Team Grey = $2 \times 11 + 4 \times -1$ or $22 - 4 = 18$ points **[1]**
Team Blue = $2 \times 13 + 7 \times -1$ or $26 - 7 = 19$ points **[1]**
Team Blue **[1]**

4. a) $4x + 24$ **[1]** b) $40x + 240$ **[1]** c) $4x^2 + 24x$ **[1]**
d) $4x^2y + 24xy$ **[1]**

5. a)
$12 + 2x + y$
$12 + x$ | $x + y$
12 | x | y

$t = 12 + 2x + y$ **[2]**
[1 mark for middle row of wall completed correctly]
b) $t = 12 + 2(3) + 4$ or $12 + 6 + 4$ **[1]**
$= 22$ **[1]**
c) $t = 12 + 2(2) - 3$ or $12 + 4 - 3$ **[1]**
$= 13$ **[1]**

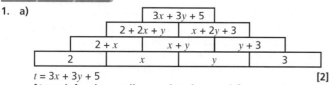

1. a)
$3x + 3y + 5$
$2 + 2x + y$ | $x + 2y + 3$
$2 + x$ | $x + y$ | $y + 3$
2 | x | y | 3

$t = 3x + 3y + 5$ **[2]**
[1 mark for three cells completed correctly]
b) $t = 3(5) + 3(2) + 5$ or $15 + 6 + 5$ **[1]**
$= 26$ **[1]**
c) $t = 3(4) + 3(4) + 5$ or $12 + 12 + 5$ **[1]**
$= 29$ **[1]**

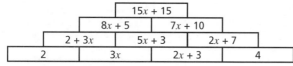

2.
$15x + 15$
$8x + 5$ | $7x + 10$
$2 + 3x$ | $5x + 3$ | $2x + 7$
2 | $3x$ | $2x + 3$ | 4

[2]
[1 mark for three cells completed correctly]

3. a)

$\times$	$2x$	1
$3x$	$6x^2$	$3x$
5	$10x$	5

[2]
[1 mark for two correct cells]
b) $6x^2 + 13x + 5$ **[1]**

Pages 35–38: Fractions

1. $\frac{5}{6}$ **[1]**

2. Divide the numerator and denominator by the same number, until they have no more common factors.

a) $\frac{2}{3}$ **[1]** b) $\frac{3}{5}$ **[1]** c) 1 **[1]** d) $\frac{43}{50}$ **[1]** e) $\frac{3}{7}$ **[1]** f) $\frac{3}{4}$ **[1]**

3. Multiply numerator by numerator and denominator by denominator. Simplify if possible.

a) $\frac{4}{5}$ **[1]** b) $\frac{1}{3}$ **[1]** c) $\frac{9}{4} = 2\frac{1}{4}$ **[1]** d) $\frac{1}{28}$ **[1]** e) $\frac{1}{24}$ **[1]**
f) $\frac{2}{15}$ **[1]** g) $\frac{5}{24}$ **[1]** h) $\frac{6}{35}$ **[1]** i) $\frac{15}{80} = \frac{3}{16}$ **[1]**

4. Convert one or both fractions so they have the same denominator before adding or subtracting.

a) $\frac{3}{5}$ **[1]** b) $2\frac{1}{6}$ **[1]** c) $\frac{2}{9}$ **[1]** d) $\frac{1}{8}$ **[1]** e) $\frac{3}{6} = \frac{1}{2}$ **[1]**
f) $\frac{7}{12}$ **[1]** g) $\frac{2}{24} = \frac{1}{12}$ **[1]** h) $\frac{13}{20}$ **[1]** i) $\frac{31}{40}$ **[1]**

5. a) $1\frac{1}{8}$ **[1]** b) $4\frac{1}{4}$ **[1]** c) $6\frac{2}{3}$ **[1]**

6. a) $\frac{5}{4}$ **[1]** b) $\frac{16}{5}$ **[1]** c) $\frac{38}{7}$ **[1]**

7. To divide by a fraction, multiply by its reciprocal. $3 = \frac{3}{1}$ so the reciprocal of 3 is $\frac{1}{3}$

a) $\frac{1}{12}$ **[1]** b) $\frac{2}{5}$ **[1]** c) $\frac{2}{18} = \frac{1}{9}$ **[1]**

8. a) $\frac{73}{100}$ **[1]** b) $\frac{284}{1000} = \frac{71}{250}$ **[1]** c) $\frac{36}{100} = \frac{9}{25}$ **[1]**

9. 85 **[1]**

1. To divide by a fraction, multiply by its reciprocal.
The reciprocal of $\frac{2}{5}$ is $\frac{5}{2}$

a) $\frac{2}{5}$ **[1]** b) $\frac{3}{4}$ **[1]** c) $\frac{5}{6}$ **[1]** d) $\frac{5}{20} = \frac{1}{4}$ **[1]**
e) $\frac{40}{42} = \frac{20}{21}$ **[1]** f) $\frac{12}{18} = \frac{2}{3}$ **[1]**

2. a) 0.7 **[1]** b) 0.23 **[1]** c) 0.409 **[1]** d) 0.25 **[1]**
e) 0.05 **[1]** f) 0.52 **[1]** g) 0.625 **[1]**
h) 0.42857142… **[1]** i) 0.2222222… **[1]**

3. $\frac{1}{6}, \frac{2}{9}, \frac{3}{7}, \frac{1}{2}, \frac{7}{11}, \frac{11}{12}$ **[2]**
[1 mark for at least four in correct order]

4. $\frac{2}{9}, \frac{1}{3}$, 0.35, $\frac{3}{4}$, 0.8, $\frac{5}{6}$ **[2]**
[1 mark for at least four in correct order]

5. a) 6 **[1]** b) 45 **[1]** c) 20 **[1]**

6. 36 **[1]**

7. a) $>$ **[1]** b) $<$ **[1]** c) $=$ **[1]** d) $<$ **[1]** e) $=$ **[1]** f) $>$ **[1]**

8. $\frac{18}{50}$ **[1]** $= \frac{9}{25}$ **[1]**

9. a) $2\frac{9}{10}$ **[1]** b) $4\frac{19}{24}$ **[1]** c) $1\frac{3}{20}$ **[1]**

1. To multiply or divide mixed numbers, first convert them to improper fractions.

a) $\frac{10}{12} = \frac{5}{6}$ **[1]** b) $\frac{102}{25} = 4\frac{2}{25}$ **[1]** c) $\frac{84}{35} = \frac{12}{5} = 2\frac{2}{5}$ **[1]**

2. $\frac{3}{7}$ **[1]**

3. $\frac{2}{3} \times \frac{1}{4} = \frac{2}{12} = \frac{1}{6}$ **[1]**

4. a) 27 **[1]** b) 108 **[1]** c) 54 **[1]**

5. $1\frac{7}{60}$ **[1]**

6. 9 sweets = $\frac{3}{8}$, 3 sweets = $\frac{1}{8}$, $8 \times 3 = 24$ **[1]**

7. $-1\frac{1}{4}, -\frac{2}{3}$, −0.6, $\frac{3}{5}$, 0.7 **[2]**
[1 mark for at least three in correct order]

Pages 39–42: Shapes and Angles

1. Kite C **[1]** Parallelogram A **[1]** Trapezium D **[1]** Rectangle B **[1]**

2. 251°, 292°, 217°, 320° **[1]**

3. a) Equilateral [1]
   b) Isosceles [1]
   c) Right-angled [1]
   d) Scalene [1]
4. $a = 117°$ **[1]** $b = 127°$ **[1]** $c = 45°$ **[1]**
5. Angles would add up to 179° **[1]**
   Should add up to 180° or 180° – 135° – 21° = 24° **[1]**
6. a) 145° **[1]** obtuse **[1]**
   b) 55° **[1]** acute **[1]**
   c) 290° **[1]** reflex **[1]**

1. $a = 124°$ **[1]** $b = 56°$ **[1]** $c = 65°$ **[1]** $d = 115°$ **[1]** $e = 40°$ **[1]** $f = 24°$ **[1]**
2. Angles add up to 180° **[1]** so ABC is a straight line **[1]**
3. **[1]**

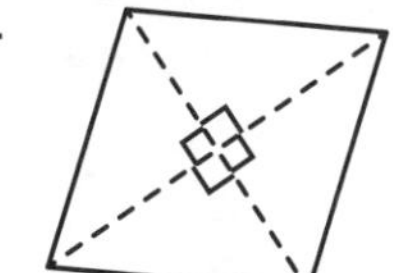

Rhombus **[1]**

4. Angles in a quadrilateral total 360° **[1]**. If $x = 124°$ then the adjacent angle = 56°. Sum of angles in the quadrilateral would therefore equal 361°, which is not possible. **[1]**

1. Square **[1]**; rectangle **[1]**
2. $a = 118°$ **[1]** $b = 62°$ **[1]** $c = 105°$ **[1]**
   $d = 131°$ **[1]** $e = 116°$ **[1]** $f = 64°$ **[1]**
3. $a = 72°$ **[1]** $b = 102°$ **[1]** $c = 16°$ **[1]**

Pages 43–47: Coordinates and Graphs

1. a) Square **[2]**
   [1 mark for plotting points and drawing the shape]
   b) Kite **[2]**
   [1 mark for plotting points and drawing the shape]

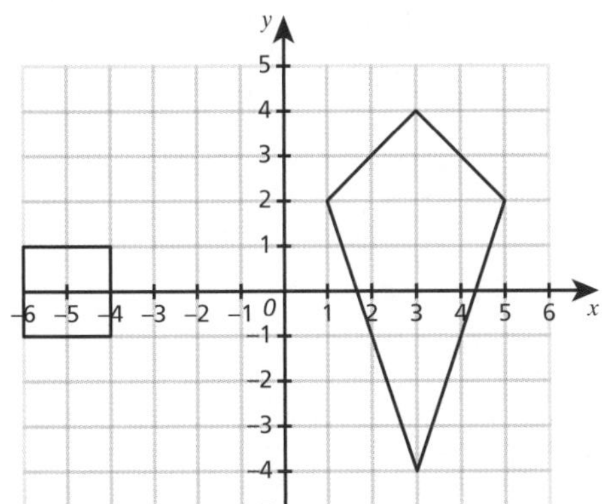

   c) Trapezium **[2]**
   [1 mark for plotting points and drawing the shape]
   d) Rectangle **[2]**
   [1 mark for plotting points and drawing the shape]

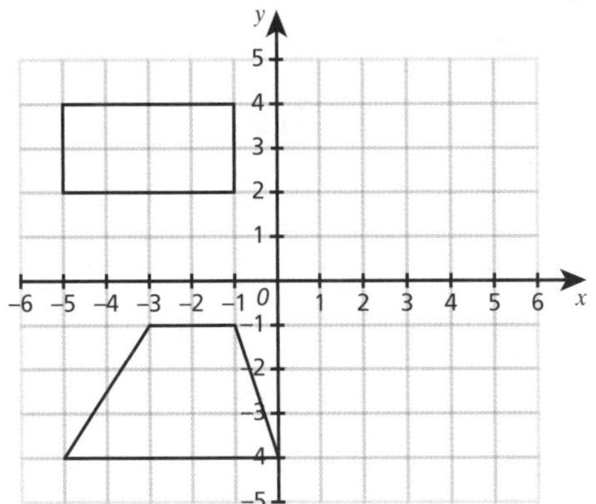

2. (1, –2) **[2]**
   [1 mark for plotting points and drawing the shape]

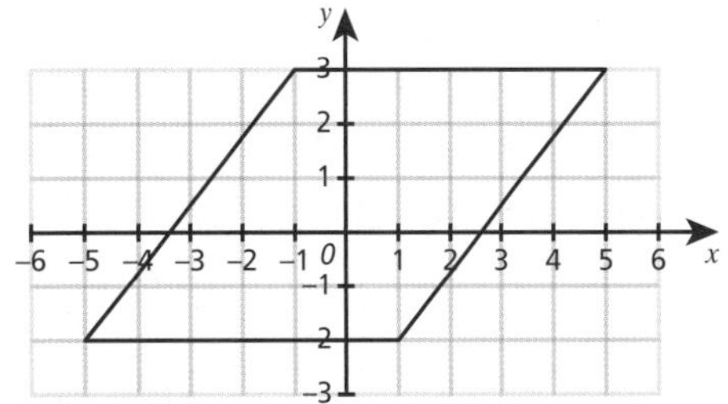

3. **A** $y = 2$ **B** $y = -1$ **C** $x = -4$ **D** $x = 0$ **E** $x = 3$ **[5]**
4. a) D and F **[1]** b) F and G **[1]** c) E **[1]** d) A **[1]**
   e) G and I **[1]** f) B and C **[1]**

1. a) JK **[1]** b) CD **[1]**
2. a)

x	0	2	4
y	**0**	**2**	**4**

[1]

b)

x	0	2	4
y	**2**	**4**	**6**

[1]

c)

x	0	2	4
y	**0**	**4**	**8**

[1]

d)

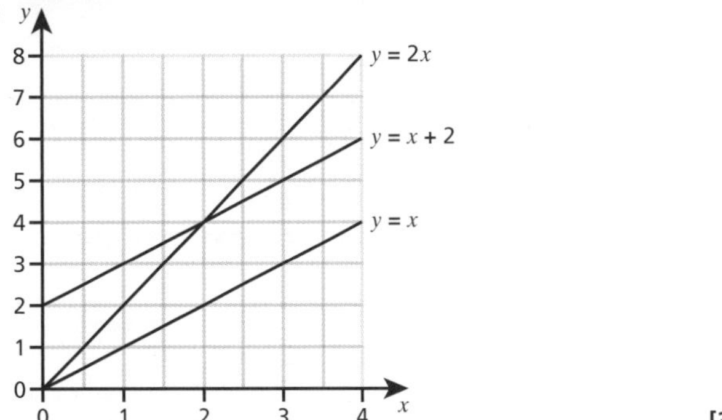

[3]

[1 mark for each correct line]

1. a) £6 **[1]** b) £24 **[1]** c) 2.5 kg **[1]**
2. a)

Euros (€)	1	10	20	30
Pounds (£)	0.90	**9**	**18**	**27**

[2]

[1 mark for two cells correct]

b)

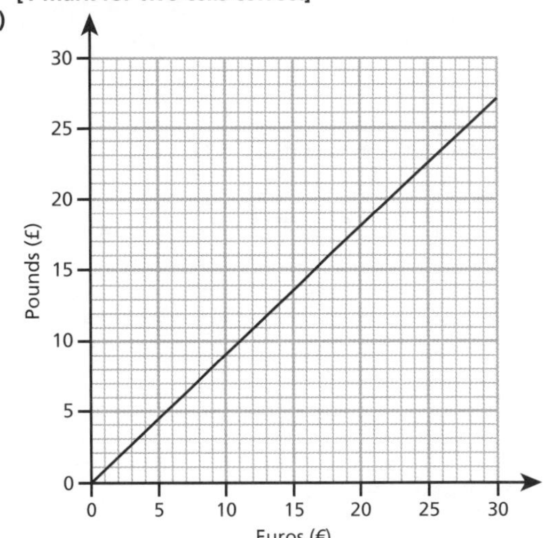

[2]

c) Reading off at €25 gives £22.50 **[1]**
d) For example, read off at £15 and multiply answer by 100 **[1]**

3. **B** $y = x + 3$ **[1]**

The y-coordinate is 3 more than the x-coordinate each time.

Pages 48–50: Percentages

1. **a)** 84% **[1]** **b)** 6% **[1]**
2. **a)** $\frac{1}{2}$ **[1]** **b)** $\frac{1}{10}$ **[1]** **c)** $\frac{1}{4}$ **[1]** **d)** $\frac{20}{100} = \frac{1}{5}$ **[1]** **e)** $\frac{3}{4}$ **[1]**
   f) $\frac{80}{100} = \frac{4}{5}$ **[1]** **g)** $\frac{46}{100} = \frac{23}{50}$ **[1]** **h)** $\frac{9}{100}$ **[1]** **i)** $\frac{8}{100} = \frac{2}{25}$ **[1]**
3. **a)** 0.35 **[1]** **b)** 0.42 **[1]** **c)** 0.6 **[1]** **d)** 0.02 **[1]**
   e) 0.375 **[1]** **f)** 0.025 **[1]**
4. **a)** 72% **[1]** **b)** 15% **[1]** **c)** 7% **[1]** **d)** 24.5% **[1]**
   e) 175% **[1]** **f)** 0.4% **[1]**
5. 20%, $\frac{2}{5}$, $\frac{1}{2}$, 65%, 0.8 **[2]**
   [1 mark for at least three in the correct order]
6. **a)** £8 **[1]** **b)** 2 kg **[1]** **c)** 2.5 m **[1]** **d)** 6 cm **[1]**
   e) 3p **[1]** **f)** 9 km **[1]**

1. **a)** £3.60 **[1]** **b)** £1.80 **[1]** **c)** £5.40 **[1]** **d)** £2.52 **[1]**
2. **a)** $\frac{13}{50} = \frac{\mathbf{26}}{100}$ = **26% [2]** **b)** $\frac{88}{200} = \frac{\mathbf{44}}{100}$ = **44% [2]**
   c) $\frac{9}{25} = \frac{\mathbf{36}}{100}$ = **36% [2]** **d)** $\frac{11}{20} = \frac{\mathbf{55}}{100}$ = **55% [2]**
3. $\frac{47}{50} = \frac{94}{100}$ = 94% **[1]**
4. **a)** $\frac{4}{25}$ = 16% **[1]** **b)** $\frac{7}{25}$ = 28% **[1]** **c)** $\frac{14}{25}$ = 56% **[1]**
5. £153 **[1]**

1. **a)** > **[1]** **b)** < **[1]** **c)** = **[1]**
2. **a)** Test A **[1]** **b)** Test B **[1]**
3. 30% of £22 = £6.60 **[1]**
4. **a)** Website X **[1]**
   b) Final cost on website X is £72; Final cost on website Y is £75
   Website X is cheaper **[1]**

Pages 51–55: Symmetry and Transformations

1.

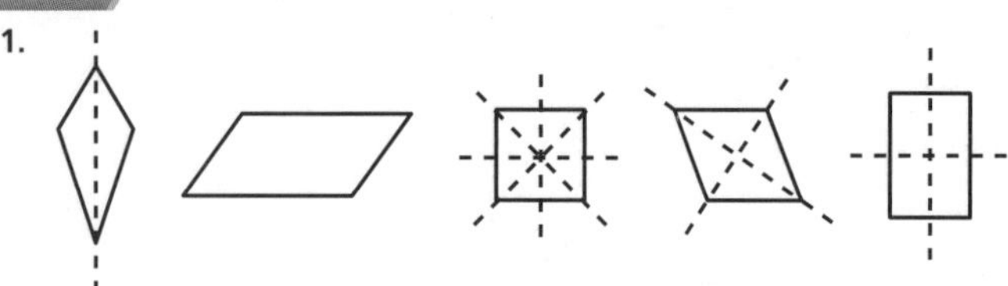

[5]

2. MA **[1]**
3.

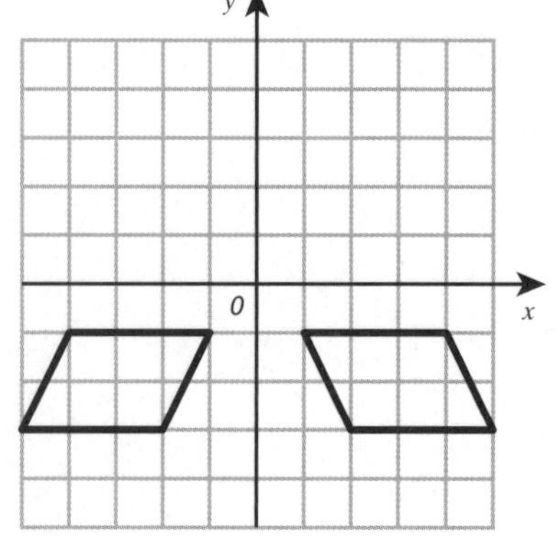

[2] **[1 mark for any reflection]**

4. 270° **[1]**

1.

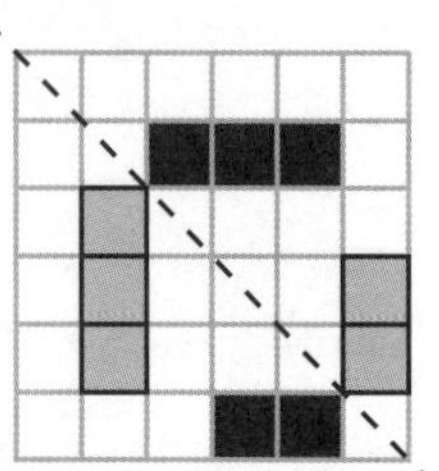

[2]

[1 mark for each rectangle]

2.

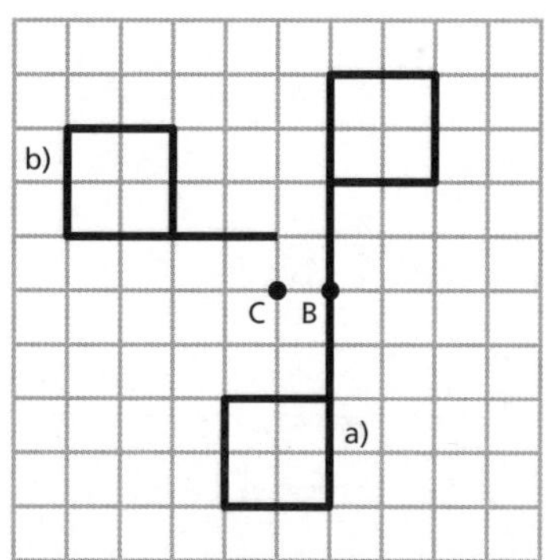

a) [2] **[1 mark for any rotation of the original shape about B]**
b) [2] **[1 mark for any 90° anti-clockwise rotation of the flag]**

Use tracing paper.

3. **a)**

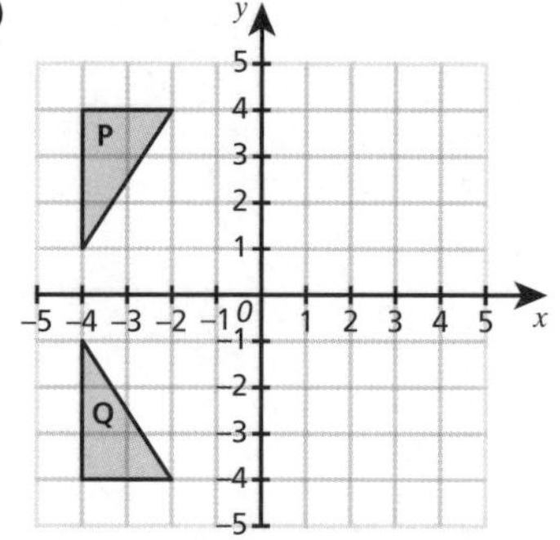

[2]

[1 mark for any reflection]
b) x-axis **[1]**
4. Centre of enlargement **[1]** and scale factor **[1]**
5. **a)** 2 units right and 2 units down **[1]**
   b) 5 units left and 1 unit down **[1]**
   c) 5 units right and 4 units up **[1]**
   d) 4 units left **[1]**

1. **a)** 2 **[1]**
   b) (–1, 2) **[1]**
2.

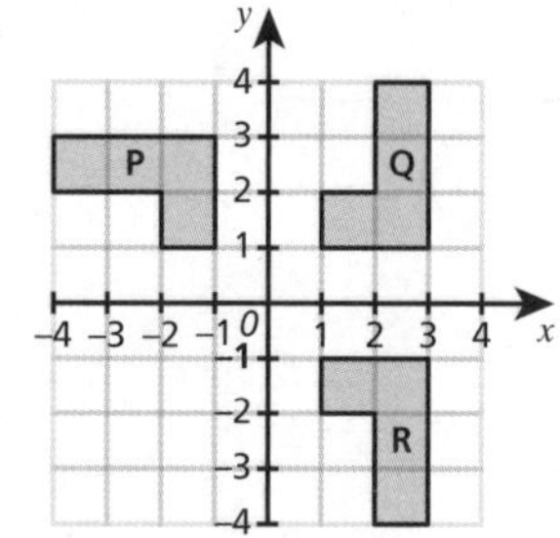

a) [2] **[1 mark for any 90° rotation]**
b) [2] **[1 mark for any reflection]**

Use tracing paper.

3. 2 units to the right and 6 units down **[1]**
4.

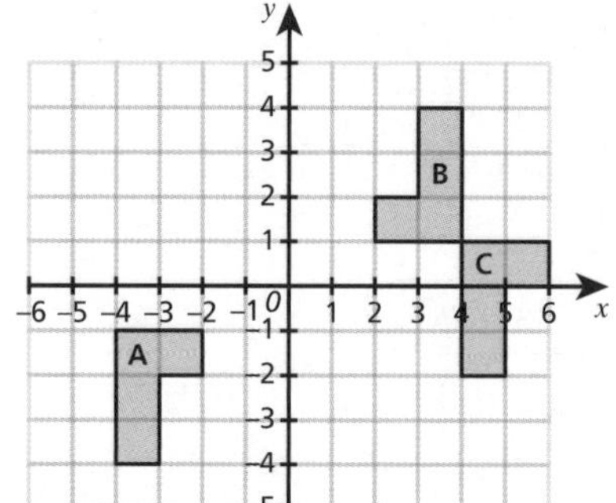

a) [2] **[1 mark for any rotation]**
b) [2] **[1 mark for any rotation]**
c) A translation of 8 units to the right and 2 units up [1]

5.

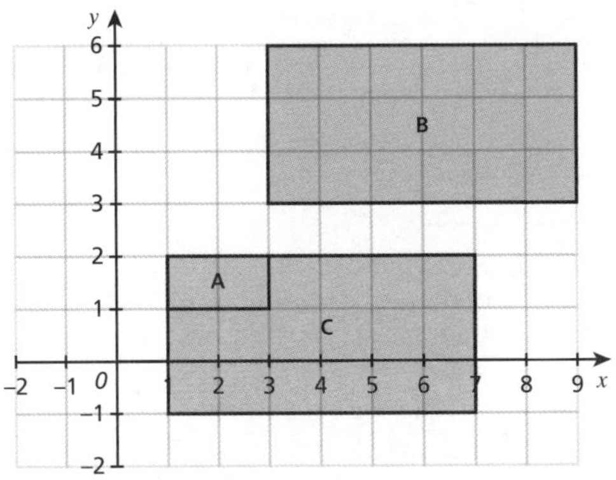

A B C

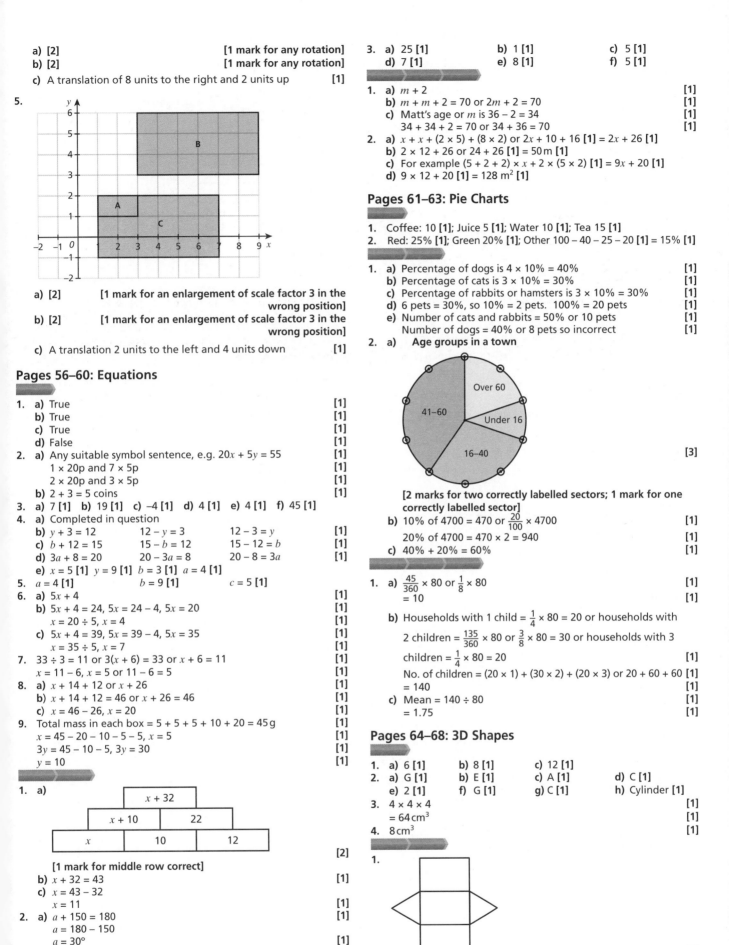

a) [2] **[1 mark for an enlargement of scale factor 3 in the wrong position]**
b) [2] **[1 mark for an enlargement of scale factor 3 in the wrong position]**
c) A translation 2 units to the left and 4 units down [1]

Pages 56–60: Equations

1. a) True [1]
   b) True [1]
   c) True [1]
   d) False [1]
2. a) Any suitable symbol sentence, e.g. $20x + 5y = 55$ [1]
   1 × 20p and 7 × 5p [1]
   2 × 20p and 3 × 5p [1]
   b) 2 + 3 = 5 coins [1]
3. a) 7 **[1]** b) 19 **[1]** c) –4 **[1]** d) 4 **[1]** e) 4 **[1]** f) 45 **[1]**
4. a) Completed in question
   b) $y + 3 = 12$ $12 - y = 3$ $12 - 3 = y$ [1]
   c) $b + 12 = 15$ $15 - b = 12$ $15 - 12 = b$ [1]
   d) $3a + 8 = 20$ $20 - 3a = 8$ $20 - 8 = 3a$ [1]
   e) $x = 5$ **[1]** $y = 9$ **[1]** $b = 3$ **[1]** $a = 4$ **[1]**
5. $a = 4$ **[1]** $b = 9$ **[1]** $c = 5$ **[1]**
6. a) $5x + 4$ [1]
   b) $5x + 4 = 24$, $5x = 24 - 4$, $5x = 20$ [1]
   $x = 20 \div 5$, $x = 4$ [1]
   c) $5x + 4 = 39$, $5x = 39 - 4$, $5x = 35$ [1]
   $x = 35 \div 5$, $x = 7$ [1]
7. $33 \div 3 = 11$ or $3(x + 6) = 33$ or $x + 6 = 11$ [1]
   $x = 11 - 6$, $x = 5$ or $11 - 6 = 5$ [1]
8. a) $x + 14 + 12$ or $x + 26$ [1]
   b) $x + 14 + 12 = 46$ or $x + 26 = 46$ [1]
   c) $x = 46 - 26$, $x = 20$ [1]
9. Total mass in each box = 5 + 5 + 5 + 10 + 20 = 45 g [1]
   $x = 45 - 20 - 10 - 5 - 5$, $x = 5$ [1]
   $3y = 45 - 10 - 5$, $3y = 30$ [1]
   $y = 10$ [1]

1. a)

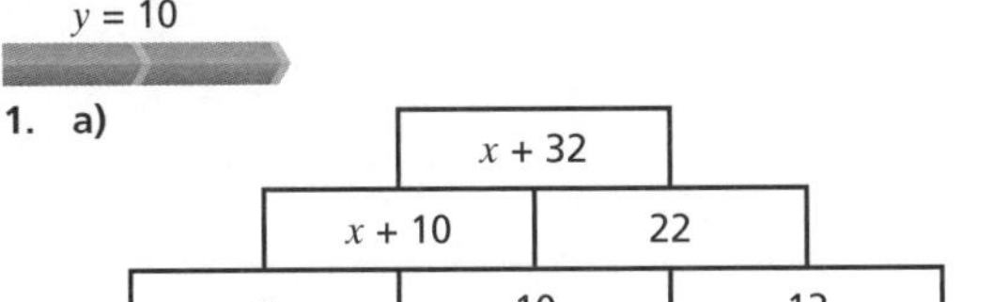

[2]

[1 mark for middle row correct]

   b) $x + 32 = 43$ [1]
   c) $x = 43 - 32$
   $x = 11$ [1]
2. a) $a + 150 = 180$ [1]
   $a = 180 - 150$
   $a = 30°$ [1]
   b) $b + 40 + 90 = 360$ or $b + 130 = 360$ [1]
   $b = 360 - 130$
   $b = 230°$ [1]
   c) $4c = 180$ [1]
   $c = 180 \div 4$
   $c = 45°$ [1]

3. a) 25 **[1]** b) 1 **[1]** c) 5 **[1]**
   d) 7 **[1]** e) 8 **[1]** f) 5 **[1]**

1. a) $m + 2$ [1]
   b) $m + m + 2 = 70$ or $2m + 2 = 70$ [1]
   c) Matt's age or m is 36 – 2 = 34 [1]
   34 + 34 + 2 = 70 or 34 + 36 = 70 [1]
2. a) $x + x + (2 \times 5) + (8 \times 2)$ or $2x + 10 + 16$ **[1]** $= 2x + 26$ **[1]**
   b) 2 × 12 + 26 or 24 + 26 **[1]** = 50 m **[1]**
   c) For example $(5 + 2 + 2) \times x + 2 \times (5 \times 2)$ **[1]** $= 9x + 20$ **[1]**
   d) 9 × 12 + 20 **[1]** = 128 m² **[1]**

Pages 61–63: Pie Charts

1. Coffee: 10 **[1]**; Juice 5 **[1]**; Water 10 **[1]**; Tea 15 **[1]**
2. Red: 25% **[1]**; Green 20% **[1]**; Other 100 – 40 – 25 – 20 **[1]** = 15% **[1]**

1. a) Percentage of dogs is 4 × 10% = 40% [1]
   b) Percentage of cats is 3 × 10% = 30% [1]
   c) Percentage of rabbits or hamsters is 3 × 10% = 30% [1]
   d) 6 pets = 30%, so 10% = 2 pets. 100% = 20 pets [1]
   e) Number of cats and rabbits = 50% or 10 pets [1]
   Number of dogs = 40% or 8 pets so incorrect [1]
2. a) **Age groups in a town**

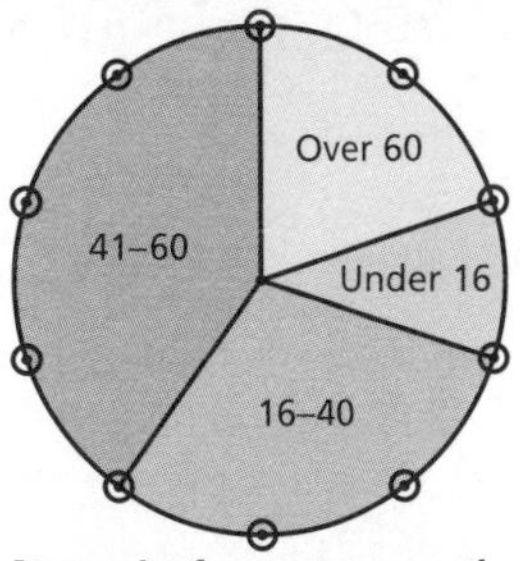

Over 60
41–60
Under 16
16–40

[3]

[2 marks for two correctly labelled sectors; 1 mark for one correctly labelled sector]

   b) 10% of 4700 = 470 or $\frac{20}{100} \times 4700$ [1]
   20% of 4700 = 470 × 2 = 940 [1]
   c) 40% + 20% = 60% [1]

1. a) $\frac{45}{360} \times 80$ or $\frac{1}{8} \times 80$ [1]
   = 10 [1]
   b) Households with 1 child = $\frac{1}{4} \times 80 = 20$ or households with 2 children = $\frac{135}{360} \times 80$ or $\frac{3}{8} \times 80 = 30$ or households with 3 children = $\frac{1}{4} \times 80 = 20$ [1]
   No. of children = (20 × 1) + (30 × 2) + (20 × 3) or 20 + 60 + 60 [1]
   = 140 [1]
   c) Mean = 140 ÷ 80 [1]
   = 1.75 [1]

Pages 64–68: 3D Shapes

1. a) 6 **[1]** b) 8 **[1]** c) 12 **[1]**
2. a) G **[1]** b) E **[1]** c) A **[1]** d) C **[1]**
   e) 2 **[1]** f) G **[1]** g) C **[1]** h) Cylinder **[1]**
3. 4 × 4 × 4 [1]
   = 64 cm³ [1]
4. 8 cm³ [1]

1.

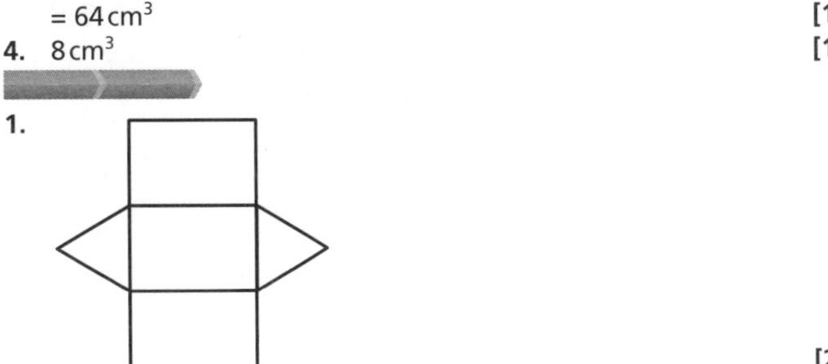

[2]

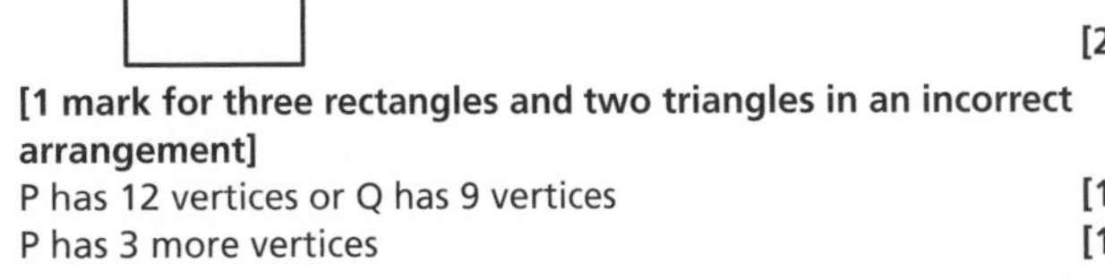

[1 mark for three rectangles and two triangles in an incorrect arrangement]

2. P has 12 vertices or Q has 9 vertices [1]
   P has 3 more vertices [1]

3. a) C [2]

Enlarge the nets and attempt to fold them into a cube.

b) A: 6 **[1]** B: 4 **[1]** D: 6 **[1]**

4. 8 vertices **[1]** 6 faces **[1]** 12 edges **[1]**

5. $8 \times 4 \times 3$ **[1]**

$= 96\,\text{cm}^3$ **[1]**

1. 8 **[1]**
2. Volume P = $5 \times 6 \times 8 = 240\,\text{cm}^3$ **[1]**
   Volume Q = $5 \times 7 \times 7 = 245\,\text{cm}^3$ **[1]**
   Q larger by $5\,\text{cm}^3$ **[1]**
3. Volume = $5 \times 6 \times 8 = 240\,\text{cm}^3$ **[1]**
   Height = 10 cm **[1]**
4. $252\,000\,\text{cm}^3$ **[1]** ÷ 50 **[1]** = 5040 seconds **[1]** = 84 minutes **[1]**

Divide by 60 to change seconds into minutes.

5. Dimensions are $5 \times 8 \times 3$ **[2]** so volume = $120\,\text{cm}^3$ **[1]**
   [1 mark for 5 × 3 or 8 × 5 or 8 × 3]

Consider factor pairs of areas and test different numbers to find the ones that work.

Pages 69–72: Ratio

1. a) Any 3 squares coloured black. 7 squares left white. **[1]**
   b) Any 4 squares coloured black. 6 squares left white. **[1]**
   c) Any 10 squares coloured black. 6 squares left white. **[1]**
2. a) Amit £6 **[1]** Bill £15 **[1]**

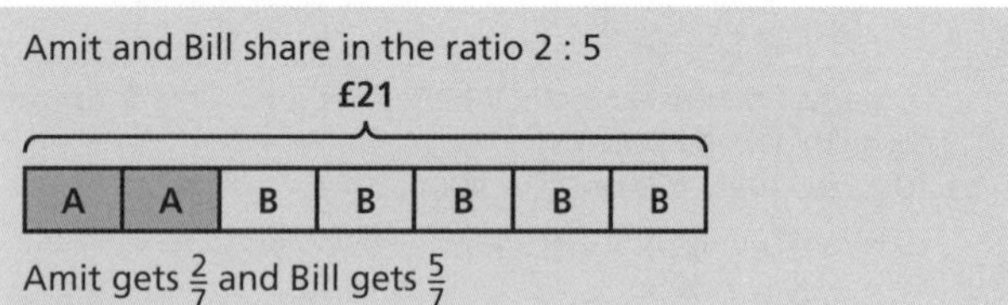

b) Cory 75 g **[1]** Daisy 125 g **[1]**

3. a) 120 ml **[1]**
   b) 210 ml **[1]**
4. a)

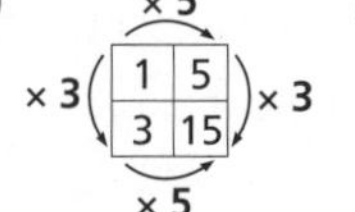

b)

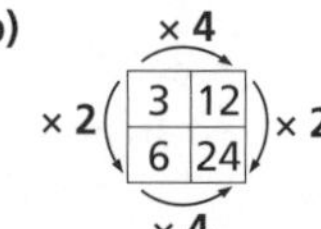

c)

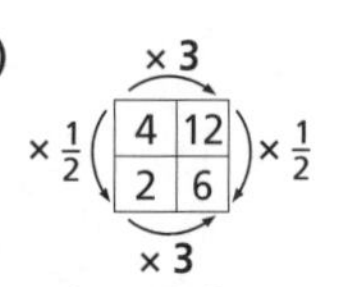

[6]

[1 mark each for horizontal multipliers; 1 mark each for vertical multipliers]

5. a) £10 **[1]**
   b) Any answer between €3.4 and €3.8 **[1]**

0 5 10
£
€
0 6 12

6. a)

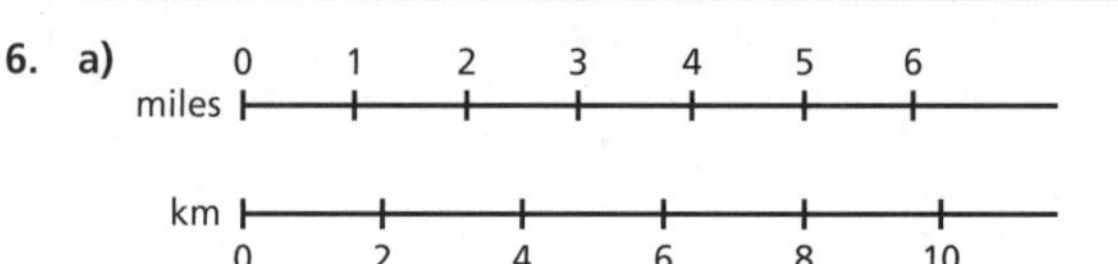

[2]

[1 mark if there are errors, but 5 miles and 8 km are correctly labelled]

b) 3 miles **[1]**

7. $\frac{7}{9}$ **[1]**

1. a) $\frac{4}{5}$ **[1]** b) $\frac{5}{4}$ **[1]** c) $\frac{5}{9}$ **[1]**

Gina and Harry share in the ratio 4 : 5

G	G	G	G	
H	H	H	H	H

2. a) ✓ **[1]** b) ✗ **[1]** c) ✗ **[1]**
3. a)

20	10	**5**
24	**12**	6

[2]

b) Ray 10 claps, Lou 12 claps **[1]**
Ray 5 claps, Lou 6 claps **[1]**
c) Ray 25 claps, Lou 30 claps **[1]**

4. Izzy gets $\frac{4}{7}$, Jake gets $\frac{3}{7}$, difference is 5 mints = $\frac{1}{7}$ **[1]**
   Jake gets $\frac{3}{7} = 3 \times 5 = 15$ mints **[1]**
5. a) 1 square black, 3 squares grey. 6 squares left white. **[2]**
   b) 3 squares black, 5 squares grey. 2 squares left white. **[2]**
   c) 2 squares black, 10 squares grey. 4 squares left white. **[2]**
   [Parts a), b) and c): 1 mark if the number of black squares or the number of grey squares is correct, but not both]

1. a) 11 pounds **[1]**
   b) 1 pound = 5 ÷ 11 = 0.454545... kg or 0.455 kg to 3 d.p. **[1]**
2. a) b)

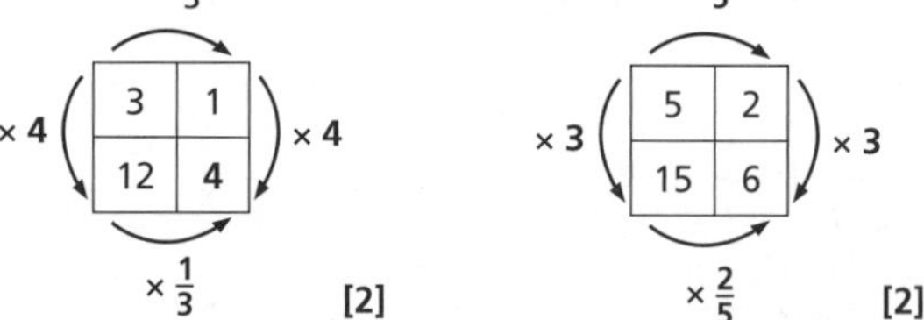

c)

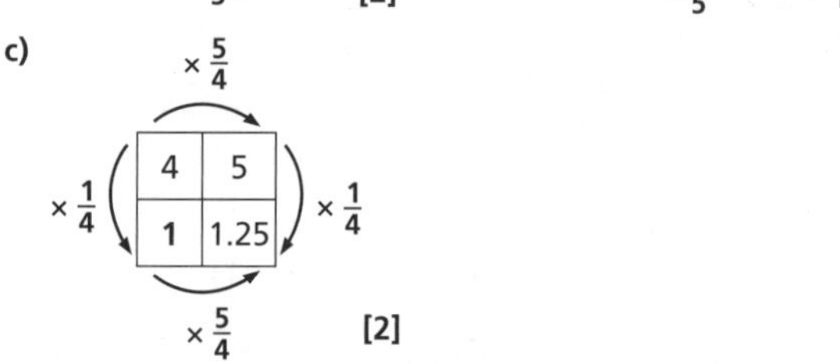

[Parts a), b) and c): 1 mark if there is one error only]

3. Max's share is 3 parts, Nora's share is 7 parts, so difference is 4 parts **[1]**
   4 parts represents 8 toffees, so 1 part represents 2 toffees **[1]**
   Nora gets $7 \times 2 = 14$ toffees **[1]**
4. 9 **[1]**
5. Oli's proportion of squash is $\frac{1}{8} = \frac{5}{40}$ **[1]**
   Polly's proportion of squash is $\frac{3}{20} = \frac{6}{40}$ **[1]**
   Polly's drink has the higher proportion of squash. **[1]**